Re-Scripting Walt Whitman

Additional praise for *Re-Scripting Walt Whitman*

"Whitman is America's ever-fluid text. Thorough, concise, and engagingly written, *Re-scripting Walt Whitman* illuminates the life and works – the poet's sexuality, politics, and ceaseless growth – with an important new emphasis on manuscripts, revision, and the innovative online *Walt Whitman Archive* that will startle general readers and literary scholars alike."

John Bryant, Hofstra University

"A splendid primer to the complexities of Whitman's prose and verse. Folsom and Price expertly trace the evolution of Whitman's career and the gradual growth of *Leaves of Grass*. Scholars no less than novices will be inspired to read Whitman with fresh insight."

Gary F. Scharnhorst, University of New Mexico

"*Re-Scripting Walt Whitman* accomplishes two significant tasks at once. It ties Whitman's poetry to his life in a clear, down-to-earth narrative of biographical detail and literary accomplishment, and it breaks new ground in its portrayal of Whitman as a *working* poet, one who knew his way around a print shop and based his radical innovations on an intimate knowledge of type, print, ink, and bookmaking. Drawing on their own experience in constructing a new electronic Whitman archive, Ed Folsom and Kenneth M. Price provide unique lessons in reading the actual materiality of Whitman's poems as the first step toward grasping their meanings."

Alan Trachtenberg, Yale University

Blackwell Introductions to Literature

1. John Milton   *Roy Flannagan*
2. Chaucer and the Canterbury Tales   *John Hirsh*
3. Arthurian Romance   *Derek Pearsall*
4. James Joyce   *Michael Seidel*
5. Mark Twain   *Stephen Railton*
6. The Modern Novel   *Jesse Matz*
7. Old Norse-Icelandic Literature   *Heather O'Donoghue*
8. Old English Literature   *Daniel Donoghue*
9. Modernism   *David Ayers*
10. Latin American Fiction   *Philip Swanson*
11. Re-Scripting Walt Whitman   *Ed Folsom and Kenneth M. Price*
12. Renaissance and Reformations   *Michael Hattaway*
13. The Art of Twentieth-Century American Literature   *Charles Altieri*

Re-Scripting Walt Whitman

An Introduction to His Life and Work

Ed Folsom and Kenneth M. Price

Blackwell
Publishing

BLACKWELL PUBLISHING
350 Main Street, Malden, MA 02148-5020, USA
9600 Garsington Road, Oxford OX4 2DQ, UK
550 Swanston Street, Carlton, Victoria 3053, Australia

The right of Ed Folsom and Kenneth M. Price to be identified
as the Authors of this Work has been asserted in accordance
with the UK Copyright, Designs, and Patents Act 1988.

First published 2005 by Blackwell Publishing Ltd

1 2005

Library of Congress Cataloging-in-Publication Data

Folsom, Ed, 1947–
Re-scripting Walt Whitman : an introduction to his life and work / Ed
    Folsom and Kenneth M. Price.
    p. cm.—(Blackwell introductions to literature)
    Includes bibliographical references and index.
    ISBN-13: 978-1-4051-1806-4 (hard cover : alk. paper)
    ISBN-13: 978-1-4051-1818-7 (pbk. : alk. paper)
    ISBN-10: 1-4051-1806-7 (hard cover : alk. paper)
    ISBN-10: 1-4051-1818-0 (pbk. : alk. paper)
1. Whitman, Walt, 1819–1892. 2. Poets, American—19th century—
    Biography. I. Price, Kenneth M. II. Title. III. Series.
    PS3231.F65 2005
    811'.3—dc22
    2004029160

A catalogue record for this title is available from the
British Library.

Set in 10/13pt Meridien
by Graphicraft Limited, Hong Kong
Printed and bound in the United Kingdom
by TJ International Ltd, Padstow, Cornwall

The publisher's policy is to use permanent paper from mills that
operate a sustainable forestry policy, and which has been
manufactured from pulp processed using acid-free and elementary
chlorine-free practices. Furthermore, the publisher ensures that
the text paper and cover board used have met acceptable
environmental accreditation standards.

For further information on
Blackwell Publishing, visit our website:
www.blackwellpublishing.com

Contents

Acknowledgments   vi
List of Abbreviations of Whitman's Works   vii
Introduction   ix

1 Growing Up in the Age of Accelerating Print:
   Whitman as Printer, Journalist, Teacher, and
   Fiction Writer   1

2 "Many Manuscript Doings and Undoings":
   The Road toward *Leaves of Grass*   17

3 "I Was Chilled with the Cold Types and Cylinder
   and Wet Paper Between Us": The First and
   Second Editions of *Leaves of Grass*   41

4 Intimate Script and the New American Bible:
   "Calamus" and the Making of the 1860 *Leaves
   of Grass*   60

5 Blood-Stained Memoranda   76

6 Reconstructing *Leaves of Grass*, Restructuring a Life   98

7 Dying into *Leaves*   117

Appendix: What Whitman Left Us   130
References   146
Index   149

Acknowledgments

Our collaboration on this book began in 1996 when we worked together on a searchable electronic scholarly resource called *Major Authors on CD-ROM: Walt Whitman* (Primary Source Media, 1997). At that time, we began tracking and writing about the evolution of *Leaves of Grass* from manuscript to print and from edition to edition. Later, we co-authored the Whitman biography for the *Dictionary of Literary Biography: Antebellum Writers in New York* (Bruccoli Clark Layman, Gale Group, 2002) and adapted it for the online biography on the *Walt Whitman Archive* (www.whitmanarchive.org). That work stands behind and informs this work.

Part of chapter 2 appeared in another form as Ed Folsom, " 'Many MS. Doings and Undoings': Walt Whitman's Writing of the 1855 *Leaves of Grass*," in Anthony Mortimer, ed., *From Wordsworth to Stevens* (Peter Lang, 2005), and part of chapter 6 appeared in another form as Ed Folsom, "Trying to Do Fair: Walt Whitman and the Good Life," *Speakeasy* (March/April 2004).

The authors want to thank the ever-growing staff of the *Whitman Archive* for their dedication, good work, and friendship. So much of what we have learned about Whitman and his work derives from the extraordinary work our colleagues and graduate students are doing every day on the *Archive*.

List of Abbreviations of Whitman's Works

AP   *An American Primer*, ed. Horace Traubel (Stevens Point, WI: Holy Cow! Press, 1987).

Corr.   *The Correspondence*, 6 vols., ed. Edwin Haviland Miller (New York: New York University Press, 1961–77); vol. 7, ed. Ted Genoways (Iowa City: University of Iowa Press, 2004).

DBN   *Daybooks and Notebooks*, 3 vols., ed. William White (New York: New York University Press, 1978).

D-T   *Drum-Taps* (New York: 1865) and *Sequel to Drum-Taps* (Washington: 1865–6). Available in facsimile as *Walt Whitman's Drum-Taps (1865) and Sequel to Drum-Taps (1865–6)*, ed. F. DeWolfe Miller (Gainesville, FL: Scholars' Facsimiles, 1959).

EPF   *Early Poems and Fiction*, ed. Thomas Brasher (New York: New York University Press, 1963).

Journ.   *The Journalism*, 2 vols., ed. Herbert Bergman, Douglas A. Noverr, and Edward J. Recchia (New York: Peter Lang, 1998–2003).

LG   *Leaves of Grass*, Comprehensive Reader's Edition, ed. Harold W. Boldgett and Sculley Bradley (New York: New York University Press, 1965).

LG 1855   *Leaves of Grass* (Brooklyn: 1855). Available in facsimile as *Leaves of Grass: A Facsimile of the First Edition* (San Francisco: Chandler, 1968).

LG 1860   *Leaves of Grass* (Boston: Thayer and Eldridge, 1860–1). Available in facsimile as *Leaves of Grass: Facsimile Edition of*

	the 1860 Text (Ithaca, NY: Cornell University Press, 1961).
LG Var.	*Leaves of Grass: A Textual Variorum of the Printed Poems,* 3 vols., ed. Sculley Bradley, Harold W. Blodgett, Arthur Golden, and William White (New York: New York University Press, 1980).
NUPM	*Notebooks and Unpublished Prose Manuscripts,* 6 vols., ed. Edward F. Grier (New York: New York University Press, 1984).
PW	*Prose Works 1892,* 2 vols., ed. Floyd Stovall (New York: New York University Press, 1963–4).
WWC	*With Walt Whitman in Camden,* by Horace Traubel, 9 vols. (various publishers, 1906–96).

Introduction

No American writer has been more influential, nationally and internationally, than Walt Whitman. Poets from his time to our own, in the United States and around the world, have talked back to Whitman, carrying on the conversation that he initiated over 150 years ago – a dialogue about democracy, poetry, love, death, and the endless permutations of life that he believed would define America and eventually produce a republic equal to its ideals.

It is difficult to become a poet in the United States without at some point coming to grips with Whitman, answering the challenge that he issued to future generations, to the "Poets to come": "I myself but write one or two indicative words for the future," he said, "Expecting the main things from you" (*LG*, 14). This continual deferral of the ideal was Whitman's style; he set in process a history and a literature that would struggle toward democracy, even if they would never fully attain it. His poetry was written to initiate response, revision, process, and his own compositional techniques emphasized his refusal to reach conclusion. Whitman was the ultimate reviser, continually reopening his poems and books to endless shuffling, retitling, editing, and reconceptualizing. *Leaves of Grass* was Whitman's title for a process more than a product: every change in his life and in his nation made him reopen his book to revision.

Whitman's desire was for a democracy that celebrated the self yet sang the ensemble, a democracy that worshipped the individual *and* the communal, that indeed defined democratic individuality as the ability to imagine and empathize with the vast variety of other individualities that composed the nation: "One's-Self I sing, a simple separate person, / Yet utter the word Democratic, the word En-Masse" (*LG*, 1). Whitman's continual wrestling with the problems and challenges of the emerging American democracy and the developing American democratic art has had a surprisingly widespread impact on other countries as well, where his democratic ideas and radical poetics have taken root and emerged in new hybrids as his work mixes with other national literatures. There are now many different Walt Whitmans at work in various poetic traditions, influencing writers in distinctive ways – in some countries he is the poet of socialism, in others the poet of spiritualism, in others still the poet of radical sexuality. His work has been translated into all the major languages of the world, and in several languages there are multiple and competing translations of *Leaves of Grass*. Even in the United States, the variety of reactions to Whitman's poetry is staggering; American poets have as often rejected him as they have embraced him. The remarkable fact is that everyone, at some point, has to confront Whitman, wrestle with his structuring of poetry, the nation, democracy, and the self: "I am large," he said, "I contain multitudes" (*LG*, 88).

From Ezra Pound and William Carlos Williams to Lawrence Ferlinghetti and Allen Ginsberg; from Langston Hughes and Jean Toomer to June Jordan and Michael Harper; from Meridel LeSueur and Muriel Rukeyser to Patricia Hampl and Sharon Olds; from D. H. Lawrence and Virginia Woolf to Charles Tomlinson and Anthony Burgess; from José Martí to Pablo Neruda and Jorge Luis Borges; from Rubén Darío, Fernando Pessoa, and Federico García Lorca to Rudolfo Anaya, Garrett Hongo, Maxine Hong Kingston, and Yusef Komunyakaa – the intense urge on the part of writers to talk back to Whitman has cut across boundaries of race, ethnicity, nationality, and gender.

This monograph has a direct relationship to our editorial work with the *Walt Whitman Archive* (www.whitmanarchive.org). That project has convinced us that a new kind of introductory book on Whitman now needs to be written. In our ongoing efforts to re-edit Whitman's work on the web, we are motivated not so much by a desire to reproduce in electronic form the many things brilliantly accomplished by the monumental *Collected Writings of Walt Whitman* (22 volumes, New York University Press, 1961–84) as by a desire to address the dated scholarship, and the gaps, peculiar orderings, errors, incoherencies, and other inadequacies, that characterize that edition. Perhaps the oddest choice made by the New York University Press editors was never to present, anywhere in the 22 volumes, a straightforward printing of the first edition of *Leaves of Grass*, a document of primary importance in literary history. In fact, with the exception of the final "deathbed" edition of *Leaves* (so called because copies were brought to Whitman during his final illness), one can only imaginatively construct the different editions from the textual notes and lists of variants in the Variorum Edition (*LG Var.*).

Another curiosity is the omission of Whitman's poetry manuscripts, an especially strange choice because the New York University Press edition includes a hefty amount of material of minor importance, meticulously edited and annotated. The three-volume Variorum Edition of *Leaves of Grass* was originally slated to present all the manuscripts, periodical publications, and book publications of Whitman's poems, but it ended up dealing only with the book publications, leaving the important manuscript origins and early periodical versions all but inaccessible. A projected second Variorum Edition, dealing with materials not accounted for in the first Variorum, has never materialized. Our electronic archive is steadily making available an increasing number of poetry manuscripts, a development that is revealing a previously unknown side of Whitman's creative process.

We therefore call our book *Re-Scripting Walt Whitman: An Introduction to His Life and Work*. Every book about Whitman, of course, rewrites the script of Whitman's life and work, altering the meaning of his work and emphasizing certain events in his life. Our book certainly re-scripts Whitman in that sense, but our title is further meant to suggest a recurring emphasis in the following pages: we are rethinking Whitman's life in terms of his script, those thousands of manuscript pages that he left behind and which, to this day, have not been adequately studied. Whitman has always been thought of as the "poet of print," the newspaperman who learned to set type and who often took his poetry manuscripts to print shops to have them set in type so that he could see immediately what they would look like on the printed page. Because of this, we often have viewed Whitman as a poet who begins and ends in print, when in fact he labored hard in script. From his early notebooks, where we can trace the first seeds of *Leaves of Grass*, through his final years, where he struggled against failing health to scribble out his last poems, Whitman's most intense struggles were in script, in that tough, originating workshop where words first meet paper. That's where the process began that resulted in Whitman's eventual identification of himself with his book.

Our book pursues the metonymic relation that Whitman famously employed between himself and his work ("this is no book, / Who touches this touches a man" [*LG*, 505]). We weave together an account of Whitman's life and an account of his works, especially his evolving masterpiece *Leaves of Grass*. In a sense, we follow Justin Kaplan's notion that "the irreducible reality of literary lives" is not the "naked self" but the "sum of a writer's public verbal acts and ecstasies with language" (Kaplan 1979, 55). Once we begin to think about Whitman through the lens provided by digital resources, new questions become accessible and new problems emerge. Certainly some of the inadequacy of older models of criticism becomes clear. Many of us still talk about "Song of Myself" as if it were a single, stable entity. Yet this poem took various forms and had various titles in the six different editions of *Leaves of Grass* from 1855 to 1881, and it had a complex pre-history in manuscripts and early notebooks. Our discussion highlights Whitman's evolving work – including the material production of the books themselves – in the context of his life. Many aspects of books that Whitman typically controlled – including typeface, margins, ornamentation, and the like – communicate in subtle but powerful ways to readers, and in ways that have been for the most part ignored.

We are looking, in other words, at Whitman's life as a writer – his *writing life*. In doing so, we emphasize his "scripted life," the manuscript origins of his work that tell us some remarkable things about his motivations, ideas, and thinking processes. We also investigate his "life in press," the ways that his training and experience as a printer and typesetter affected his evolving belief that he could literally transfer his identity to the printed page, embody himself in books. Our narrative attempts to illuminate both Whitman's life and his work by focusing on those places where they most thoroughly meld.

We begin with a consideration of what it meant to grow up in the age of accelerating print. Whitman's childhood took place in and around New York City, which at the time was experiencing an explosion in print technology and printed products. From his schooling through his newspaper apprenticeships, Whitman was formed in key ways by the technological developments that made cheap paper and cheap printing accessible to the quickly expanding population of the

US. As a young teenager, Whitman was already publishing professional written work. He was surrounded by a vibrant and chaotic newspaper- and book-publishing world, where the very nature of a genre like "poetry" was morphing before his eyes. He was an aspiring fiction writer, journalist, and poet. As a schoolteacher, he was fascinated by the new development of school textbooks, and he had much to say about the kinds of books America should be having its young people read. There are ways, in fact, to see the first edition of *Leaves of Grass* (which begins with a poem about a child asking a deceptively simple question – "What is the grass?" – and features a poem about the education of a child who went forth into the world) as a kind of poetic textbook.

Our second chapter, "'Many Manuscript Doings and Undoings,'" looks at the mystery years leading up to the first edition of *Leaves of Grass* and explores the little-known manuscript sources of that book. We examine in detail some of his notebooks and manuscript jottings in which *Leaves* was born, and we explore how those manuscripts teach us a great deal about Whitman's poetry – its forms, its compositional process, its meanings.

Our third chapter treats Whitman's first two editions of *Leaves* (1855, 1856). These were possibly Whitman's most radical editions, at once challenging publishing conventions and creating new conventions. Examining these editions in their material, aesthetic, and ideological aspects opens a window into Whitman's thinking as a thirty-something newspaper man who was groping for a new genre to express his radical notions of democracy, reading, writing, and absorptive American identity.

"Intimate Script and the New American Bible," our fourth chapter, examines the years from 1856 to the publication of Whitman's 1860 edition of *Leaves*. These years, too, are still something of a mystery, involving the haunting and intimate manuscript cycle of male–male love poems that he never published but instead reworked into a much more public statement of camaraderie that became a centerpiece of the edition of *Leaves* that he construed to be an "American Bible." The wild swings between private and public, personal love and public love, script and print, that mark this era of his life are indicative of a fermenting imagination that was seeking a way to fuse the personal and public, to make the act of reading at once the most public act in America (everyone reading the same thing) and the most intimate (each reader penetrated by the words of the author whose book was held in hand).

The Civil War changed everything for Whitman, including the nature and purpose of writing, as we attempt to show in chapter 5, "Blood-Stained Memoranda." His never-published manuscript notebooks written during the war are some of the most astonishing Civil War documents extant. Whitman did not think of himself primarily as a poet, but rather as a writer, and his work always probes the borders between prose and poetry, fiction and nonfiction, realism and romanticism. His work is at its most radical when he finds the conduits and seepages that allow him to explore ideas and events in genre-breaking ways. The Civil War notebooks, out of which grow his poems *Drum-Taps* and his prose *Memoranda During the War*, are the workshop where we can see the poems when they were still prose, can trace the prose becoming poems, and can experience his life among the wounded soldiers in hospitals becoming words, occasionally literally stained by the blood of the young men he was nursing.

In the American Reconstruction period, Whitman engaged in his own process of "Reconstructing *Leaves of Grass*," the subject of our sixth chapter. As the nation was reconstructing itself politically and healing from the war, Whitman undertook the complete reordering and rebuilding of *Leaves of Grass*. The 1867 edition literally sewed in his Civil War poems, and by 1870 he had made *Leaves* almost unrecognizably different from its pre-war state. His prose work during this time, notably *Democratic Vistas*, serves as a companion to this rebuilding project.

"Dying into *Leaves*" treats the last decade of Whitman's life, a period often ignored by critics and biographers. This is in fact an illuminating and active period for Whitman, as he once again enters into a series of experiments in merging prose and poetry. He publishes two books that run the genres together, and he oversees the production of a single volume that gathers his prose and poetry. He incorporates *Memoranda During the War* into a wildly suggestive new kind of autobiographical prose that he names *Specimen Days*, capturing his sense of identity as a series of indicative and often contradictory moments instead of a clear unity.

Whitman's life created a chaos of words, printed and unprinted, finished and barely begun. In an appendix, called "What Whitman Left Us," we examine the history of how his work has been categorized and printed and taught, and we look at how that history suggests the various purposes to which Whitman has been put over the last century. From the 1902 Camden edition of his *Complete Writings* to the New York University Press 22-volume scholarly edition of his *Collected Writings* to the new *Whitman Archive* on the Internet, the story of how we gather and sort and label and categorize this massive life-in-words tells us a great deal about how we have read Whitman's significance, and it indicates the new ways we may read him in the future.

CHAPTER 1

Growing Up in the Age of Accelerating Print: Whitman as Printer, Journalist, Teacher, and Fiction Writer

Walt Whitman, arguably America's most influential and innovative poet, was born into a working-class family in West Hills, New York, a village near Hempstead, Long Island, on May 31, 1819, just 30 years after George Washington was inaugurated as the first president of the newly formed United States. When Whitman was born, the new country was still very much in formation. Only five years before the poet's birth, the United States Capitol Building, the White House, the Library of Congress, and other key governmental buildings in Washington had been burned by the British in the War of 1812, a war that most Americans did not want to fight, and the purposes of which seemed as amorphous to many citizens then as they do to students of American history today. Andrew Jackson, however, emerged as a wildly popular figure after he led American troops to victory in the battle of New Orleans that ended the war. Jackson would soon turn his attention to conquering Spanish Florida – and the Seminole Indians and escaped black slaves who fought with Spain – and claiming it for the US.

As Whitman entered the world, the US Congress was just beginning to meet again in the reconstructed Capitol Building. But Congress, like the nation, was already torn in fierce debate over the issue of slavery, and within the first year of Whitman's life, the Missouri Compromise was enacted, part of the tormented balancing act between slave and free states that would define so much of the nation's history while Whitman was growing up, a tension that would culminate in the Civil War. Virtually all of the political issues that would occupy Whitman during his lifetime, and that would inspire and inform his poetry, were gestating at the time of his birth.

Walt Whitman was named after his father, a carpenter and farmer who was 34 years old when Whitman was born. Walter Sr had been born just after the end of the American Revolution; always a liberal thinker, he knew and admired Thomas Paine. Trained as a carpenter but struggling to find work, Walter Sr had taken up farming by the time Walt was born, but when Walt was just about to turn four, Walter Sr moved the family to the growing city of Brooklyn, across from New York City, or "Mannahatta" as Whitman would come to call it in his celebratory writings about the city that was just then emerging as the nation's major urban center. One of Walt's favorite stories about his childhood concerned the time General Lafayette visited New York and, selecting the 6-year-old Walt from a crowd in Brooklyn, lifted him up and carried him. Whitman later came to view this event as a kind of laying on of hands, the French hero of the American Revolution anointing the future poet of democracy in the energetic city of immigrants, where the new nation was being invented day by day.

Walt Whitman is thus of the first generation of Americans who were born in the newly formed United States and grew up assuming the existence of a unified new country. Despite the nation's many problems, pride in the United States was rampant, and Walter Sr – after giving his first son Jesse (1818–70) his own father's name, his second son his own name, his daughter Mary (1822–99) the name of Walt's maternal great-grandmother, and his daughter Hannah (1823–08) the name of his own mother – turned to the heroes of the Revolution and the War of 1812 for the names of his other three sons: Andrew Jackson Whitman (1827–63), George Washington Whitman (1829–1901), and Thomas Jefferson Whitman (1833–90). Only the youngest son, Edward (1835–1902), who was mentally and physically handicapped, carried a name that tied him to neither the family's nor the country's history.

Walter Whitman Sr was of English stock, and his marriage in 1816 to Louisa Van Velsor, of Dutch and Welsh stock, led to what Walt always considered a fertile tension in the Whitman children between a more smoldering, brooding Puritanical temperament and a sunnier, more outgoing Dutch disposition. Whitman's father was a stern and sometimes hot-tempered man, maybe an alcoholic, whom Whitman respected but for whom he never felt a great deal of affection. His mother, on the other hand, served throughout his life as his emotional touchstone. There was a special affectional bond between Whitman and his mother, and the long correspondence between them records a kind of partnership in attempting to deal with the family crises that mounted over the years, as Jesse became mentally unstable and violent and eventually had to be institutionalized, as Hannah entered a disastrous marriage with an abusive husband, as Andrew became an alcoholic and married a prostitute before dying of ill health in his thirties, and as Edward required increasingly dedicated care.

During Walt's childhood, the Whitman family moved around Brooklyn a great deal as Walter Sr tried, mostly unsuccessfully, to cash in on the city's quick growth by speculating in real estate – buying an empty lot, building a house, moving his family in, then trying to sell it at a profit to start the whole process over again. Walt loved living close to the East River, where as a child he rode the ferries back and forth to New York City, imbibing an experience that would remain significant for him his whole life: he loved ferries and the people who worked on them, and his 1856 poem eventually entitled "Crossing Brooklyn Ferry" explored the full resonance of the experience. The act of crossing became, for Whitman, one of the most evocative events in his life – at once practical, enjoyable, and mystical. The daily commute suggested the passage from life to death to life again and suggested too the passage from poet to reader to poet via the vehicle of the poem. By crossing Brooklyn ferry, Whitman first discovered the magical commutations that he would eventually accomplish in his poetry.

While in Brooklyn, Whitman attended the newly founded Brooklyn public schools for six years, sharing his classes with students of a variety of ages and backgrounds, though most were poor, since children from wealthier families generally attended private schools. In Whitman's school, all the students were in the same room, except African Americans, who had to attend a separate class on the top floor. Whitman had little to say about his rudimentary formal schooling, except that he hated corporal punishment, a common practice in schools and one that he would attack in later years in both his journalism and his fiction. But most of Whitman's meaningful education came outside of school, when he visited museums, went to libraries, and attended lectures. He always recalled the first great lecture he heard, when he was 10 years old, given by the radical Quaker leader Elias Hicks, an acquaintance of Whitman's father and a close friend of Whitman's grandfather Jesse. While Whitman's parents were not members of any religious denomination, Quaker thought always played a major role in Whitman's life, in part because of the early influence of Hicks, and in part because his mother Louisa's family had a Quaker background. Whitman's grandmother Amy Williams Van Velsor was especially committed to her Quaker beliefs, and her death – the same year Whitman first heard Hicks – hit young Walt hard, since he had spent many happy days at the farm of his grandmother and colorful grandfather, Major Cornelius Van Velsor.

Visiting his grandparents on Long Island was one of Whitman's favorite boyhood activities, and during those visits he developed his lifelong love of the Long Island shore, sensing the mystery of that territory where water meets land, fluid melds with solid. One of Whitman's greatest poems, "Out of the Cradle Endlessly Rocking," is on one level a reminiscence of his boyhood on the Long Island shore and of how his desire to be a poet arose in that landscape. The idyllic Long Island countryside formed a sharp contrast to the crowded energy of the quickly growing Brooklyn–New York City urban center. Whitman's experiences as a young man alternated between the city and the Long Island countryside, and he was attracted to both ways of life. This dual allegiance can be traced in his poetry, which is often marked by shifts between rural and urban settings.

By the age of 11, Whitman was done with his formal education (by this time he had far more schooling than either of his parents had received), and he began his life as a laborer, working first as an office boy for some prominent Brooklyn lawyers, who gave him a subscription to a circulating library, where his self-education began. Always an autodidact, Whitman absorbed an eclectic but wide-ranging education through his visits to museums, his nonstop reading, and his penchant for engaging everyone he met in conversation and debate. While most other major writers of his time enjoyed highly structured, classical educations at private institutions, Whitman forged his own rough and informal curriculum of literature, theater, history,

geography, music, and archeology out of the developing public resources of America's fastest-growing city.

In 1831, Whitman became an apprentice on the Long Island *Patriot*,
a liberal, working-class newspaper, where he learned the printing
trade and was first exposed to the excitement of putting words into
print, observing how thought and event could be quickly transformed
into language and immediately communicated to thousands of readers.
At the age of 12, young Walt was already contributing to the newspaper
and experiencing the exhilaration of getting his own words published.
Whitman's first signed article, in the fashionable New York *Mirror* in
1834, expressed his amazement at how there were still people alive
who could remember "the present great metropolitan city as a little
dorp or village; all fresh and green as it was, from its beginning," and
he wrote of a slave, "Negro Harry," who had died in 1758 at age 120
and who could remember New York "when there were but three houses
in it" (*Journ.*, 1:3). Here, at age 15, Whitman was already exploring
subjects – his city's and his nation's remarkable growth and heterogeneous population – that would continue to fascinate him throughout
his career as a writer. Even late in his life, he could still recall the
excitement of seeing this first article in print: "How it made my heart
double-beat to see *my piece* on the pretty white paper, in nice type"
(*PW*, 1:287). For his entire life, he would maintain this fascination
with the materiality of printed objects, with the way his voice and
identity could be embodied in type and paper.

Living away from home – the rest of his family moved back to the
West Hills area in 1833, leaving 14-year-old Walt alone in the city –
and learning how to set type under the *Patriot*'s foreman printer
William Hartshorne, Whitman was gaining skills and experiencing an
independence that would mark his whole career: he would always
retain a typesetter's concern for how his words looked on a page,
what typeface they were dressed in, what effects various spatial
arrangements had, and he would always retain his stubborn independence, remaining a bachelor and living alone for most of his life.
These early years on his own in Brooklyn and New York remained
a formative influence on his writing, for it was during this time that
he developed the habit of close observation of the ever-shifting
panorama of the city, and a great deal of his future poetry and prose
came to focus on catalogs of urban life and the history of New York
City, Brooklyn, and Long Island.

Walt's brother Thomas Jefferson, known to everyone in the family as "Jeff," was born during the summer of 1833, soon after his family had resettled on a farm and only weeks after Walt had joined the crowds in Brooklyn that warmly welcomed the newly re-elected president, Andrew Jackson. Brother Jeff, 14 years younger than Walt, would become the sibling he felt closest to, their bond formed when they traveled together to New Orleans in 1848, when Jeff was about the same age as Walt was when Jeff was born. But while Jeff was a young child, Whitman spent little time with him. Walt remained separated from his family and furthered his education by absorbing the power of language from a variety of sources: various circulating libraries (where he read Sir Walter Scott, James Fenimore Cooper, and other romance novelists), theaters (where he fell in love with Shakespeare's plays and saw Junius Booth, John Wilkes Booth's father, play the title role in *Richard III*, always Whitman's favorite play), and lectures (where he heard, among others, Frances Wright, the Scottish radical emancipationist and women's rights advocate). By the time he was 16, Walt was a journeyman printer and compositor in New York City. His future career seemed set in the newspaper and printing trades, but then two of New York's worst fires wiped out the major printing and business centers of the city, and, in the midst of a dismal financial climate, Whitman retreated to rural Long Island, joining his family at Hempstead in 1836. He was only 17, but this five-year veteran of the printing trade was already on the verge of a career change.

His unlikely next career was that of a teacher. Although his own formal education was, by today's standards, minimal, his work as a newspaper apprentice had helped him develop the skills of reading and writing, more than enough for the kind of teaching he would find himself doing over the next few years. He knew he did not want to become a farmer, and he rebelled at his father's attempts to get him to work on the new family farm. Teaching was therefore an escape but was also clearly a job he was forced to take in bad economic times, and some of the unhappiest times of his life were these five years when he taught school in at least 10 different Long Island towns, rooming in the homes of his students, teaching three-month terms to large and heterogeneous classes (some with over 80 students, ranging in age from 5 to 15, for up to nine hours a day), getting very little pay, and having to put up with some very unenlightened people.

After the excitement of Brooklyn and New York, these often isolated Long Island towns depressed Whitman, and he recorded his disdain for country people in a series of letters (not discovered until the 1980s) that he wrote to a friend named Abraham Leech: "Never before have I entertained so low an idea of the beauty and perfection of man's nature, never have I seen humanity in so degraded a shape, as here," he wrote from Woodbury in 1840: "Ignorance, vulgarity, rudeness, conceit, and dulness are the reigning gods of this deuced sink of despair" (*Corr.*, 7:3).

The little evidence we have of his teaching (mostly from short recollections by a few former students) suggests that Whitman employed what were then progressive techniques – encouraging students to think aloud rather than simply recite, refusing to use corporal punishment, involving his students in educational games, and joining his students in baseball and card games. He did not hesitate to use his own poems – which he was by this time writing with some frequency, though they were rhymed, conventional verses that indicated nothing of the innovative poetry to come – as texts in his classroom. While he would continue to write frequently about educational issues and would always retain a keen interest in how knowledge is acquired, he was clearly not suited to life as a country teacher. One of the poems in his first edition of *Leaves of Grass*, eventually called "There Was a Child Went Forth," can be read as a statement of Whitman's educational philosophy, celebrating unrestricted extracurricular learning and an openness to experience and ideas that would allow for endless absorption of variety and difference: this was the kind of education Whitman had given himself and the kind he valued. He would always be suspicious of classrooms, and his great poem "Song of Myself" is generated by a child's wondering question, "What is the grass?," a question that Whitman spends the rest of the poem ruminating about as he discovers the complex in the seemingly simple, the cosmos in himself – an attitude that is possible, he says, only when we put "creeds and schools in abeyance." He kept himself alive intellectually by taking an active part in debating societies and in political campaigns: inspired by the Scottish reformist Frances Wright, who came to the United States to support Martin Van Buren in the presidential election of 1836, Whitman became an industrious worker for the Democratic party, campaigning hard for Van Buren's successful candidacy.

By 1841, Whitman's second career was at an end. He had interrupted his teaching in 1838 to try his luck at starting his own newspaper, the *Long Islander*, devoted to covering the towns around Huntington. He bought a press and type and hired his younger brother George as an assistant, but, despite his energetic efforts to edit, publish, write for, and deliver the new paper, it struggled financially, and he reluctantly returned to the classroom. Newspaper work made him happy, but teaching did not, and two years later, he abruptly quit his job as an itinerant schoolteacher and never returned to the classroom. The reasons for his decision continue to interest biographers. One persistent but unsubstantiated rumor has it that Whitman committed sodomy with one of his students while teaching in Southold, though it is not possible to prove that Whitman actually even taught there. The rumor suggests he was run out of town in disgrace, never to return and soon to abandon teaching altogether. But in fact Whitman did travel again to Southold, writing some remarkably unperturbed journalistic pieces about the place in the late 1840s and early 1860s. It seems far more likely that Whitman gave up schoolteaching because he found himself temperamentally unsuited for it. And, besides, he now had a new career opening up: he decided to become a fiction writer. Best of all, to nurture that career, he would need to return to New York City and re-establish himself in the world of journalism, since most fiction at the time was published in magazines and newspapers.

How ambitious was Whitman as a writer of short fiction? The evidence suggests that he was definitely more than a casual dabbler and that he threw himself energetically into composing stories. Still, he did not give himself over to fiction with the kind of life-changing commitment he would later give to experimental poetry. He was adding to his accomplishments, moving beyond being a respectable journalist and developing literary talents and aspirations. About twenty different newspapers and magazines printed Whitman's fiction and early poetry. His best years for fiction were between 1840 and 1845, when he placed his stories in a range of magazines, including the *American Review* (later called the *American Whig Review*) and the *Democratic Review*, one of the nation's most prestigious literary magazines. As a writer of fiction, he lacked the impulse toward innovation and the commitment to self-training that later moved him toward experimental verse, even though we can trace in his fiction some of the themes that would later flourish in *Leaves of Grass*.

His early stories are captivating in large part because they address obliquely (not to say crudely) important professional and psychological matters. His first published story, "Death in the School-Room," grew out of his teaching experience and interjected direct editorializing commentary: the narrator hopes that the "many ingenious methods of child-torture, will [soon] be gazed upon as a scorn'd memento of an ignorant, cruel, and exploded doctrine." This tale had a surprise ending: the teacher flogs a student he thinks is sleeping only to make the macabre discovery that he has been beating a corpse. Another story, "The Shadow and the Light of a Young Man's Soul," offered a barely fictionalized account of Whitman's own circumstances and attitudes: the hero, Archibald Dean, left New York because of the great fire to take charge of a small district school, a move that made him feel "as though the last float-plank which buoyed him up on hope and happiness, was sinking, and he with it." Other stories concern themselves with friendships between older and younger men (especially younger men who are weak or in need of defense since they are misunderstood and at odds with figures of authority).

Whitman's steady stream of stories in the *Democratic Review* in 1842 – he published five between January and September – must have made Park Benjamin, editor of the *New World* newspaper, conclude that Whitman was the perfect candidate to write a novel that would speak to the booming temperance movement. Whitman had earlier worked for Benjamin as a printer, and the two had quarreled, leading Whitman to write "Bamboozle and Benjamin," an article attacking this irascible editor, whose practice of rapidly printing advance copies of novels, typically by English writers, threatened both the development of native writers and the viability of US publishing houses. But now both men were willing to overlook past differences in order to seize a good financial opportunity.

In an extra number in November 1842, Benjamin's *New World* published Whitman's *Franklin Evans; or The Inebriate*. The novel centers on a country boy who, after falling prey to drink in the big city, eventually causes the deaths of three women. The plot, which ends in a conventional moralistic way, was typical of temperance literature in allowing sensationalism into literature under a moral guise. Whitman's treatment of romance and passion here, however, is unpersuasive and seems to confirm a remark he had made two years earlier that he knew nothing about women from either "experience or observation."

The novel stands nonetheless as one of the earliest explorations in American literature of the theme of miscegenation, and its treatment of the enslaved (white) body, captive to drink, has resonance, as does the novel's fascination with "fatal pleasure," Evans's name for the strong attraction many feel for sinful experience, be it drink or sex.

Interestingly, *Franklin Evans* sold more copies (approximately 20,000) than anything else Whitman published in his lifetime. The work succeeded despite being a patched-together concoction of hastily composed new writing and previously composed stories. Whitman claimed he completed *Franklin Evans* in three days and that he composed parts of the novel in the reading room of Tammany Hall, inspired by gin cocktails (another time he claimed he was buoyed by a bottle of port). He eventually described *Franklin Evans* as "damned rot – rot of the worst sort." Despite these old-age remarks, Whitman's original purpose was serious, for he supported temperance consistently in the 1840s, including in two tales – "Wild Frank's Return" and "The Child's Champion" – that turn on the consequences of excessive drinking. Moreover, Whitman began another temperance novel (*The Madman*) within months of finishing *Franklin Evans*, though he soon abandoned the project. His concern with the temperance issue may have derived from his father's drinking habits or even from Whitman's own drinking tendencies when he was an unhappy schoolteacher. Whatever the source, his concern with the issue remained throughout his career, and his poetry records, again and again, the waste of alcoholic abuse, the awful "law of drunkards" that produces "the livid faces of drunkards," "those drunkards and gluttons of so many generations," the "drunkard's breath," the "drunkard's stagger," "the old drunkard staggering home."

During the time he was writing temperance fiction, Whitman remained a generally successful journalist. He cultivated a fashionable appearance: William Cauldwell, an apprentice who knew him as lead editor at the New York *Aurora*, said that Whitman "usually wore a frock coat and high hat, carried a small cane, and the lapel of his coat was almost invariably ornamented with a boutonniere." In 1842 and 1843 he moved easily in and out of positions (as was then common among journalists) on an array of newspapers, including, in addition to the *Aurora*, the New York *Evening Tattler*, the New York *Statesman*, and the New York *Sunday Times*. And he wrote on topics ranging from criticizing how the police rounded up prostitutes to denouncing Bishop

John Hughes for his effort to use public funds to support parochial schools.

Whitman left New York in 1845, perhaps because of financial uncertainty resulting from his fluctuating income. He returned to Brooklyn and to steadier work in a somewhat less competitive journalistic environment. Often regarded as a New York City writer, his residence and professional career in the city actually ended, then, a full decade before the first appearance of *Leaves of Grass*. However, even after his move to Brooklyn, he remained connected to New York: he shuttled back and forth via the Fulton ferry, and he drew imaginatively on the city's rich and varied splendor for his subject matter.

Opera was one of the many attractions that encouraged Whitman's frequent returns to New York. In 1846 Whitman began attending performances, often with his brother Jeff, a practice that was disrupted only by the onset of the Civil War (and even during the war, he managed to attend operas whenever he got back to New York). Whitman loved the thought of the human body as its own musical instrument, and his fascination with voice would later manifest itself in his desire to be an orator and in his frequent inclusion of oratorical elements in his poetry. For Whitman, listening to opera had the intensity of a "love-grip." In particular, the great coloratura soprano Marietta Alboni sent him into raptures: throughout his life she would remain his standard for great operatic performance, and his poem "To a Certain Cantatrice" addresses her as the equal of any hero. Whitman once said, after attending an opera, that the experience was powerful enough to initiate a new era in a person's development. When he later composed a poem describing his dawning sense of vocation ("Out of the Cradle Endlessly Rocking"), opera provided both structure and contextual clues to meaning.

By the mid-1840s, Whitman had a keen awareness of the cultural resources of New York City and probably had more inside knowledge of New York journalism than anyone else in Brooklyn. The *Long Island Star* recognized his value as a journalist and, once he resettled in Brooklyn, quickly arranged to have him compose a series of editorials, two or three a week, from September 1845 to March 1846. With the death of William Marsh, the editor of the *Brooklyn Eagle*, Whitman became chief editor of that paper (he served from March 5, 1846, to January 18, 1848). He dedicated himself to journalism in these years and published little of his own poetry and fiction. However, he introduced literary reviewing to the *Eagle*, and he commented, if often superficially, on writers such as Thomas Carlyle and Ralph Waldo Emerson, who in the next decade would both have a significant impact on *Leaves of Grass*. The editor's role gave Whitman a platform from which to comment on various issues, from street lighting to politics, from banking to poetry. But Whitman claimed that what he most valued was not the ability to promote his opinions, but rather something more intimate, the "curious kind of sympathy . . . that arises in the mind of a newspaper conductor with the public he serves. He gets to *love* them."

For Whitman, to serve the public was to frame issues in accordance with working-class interests – and for him this usually meant *white* working-class interests. He sometimes dreaded slave labor as a "black tide" that could overwhelm white working men. He was adamant that slavery should not be allowed into the new western territories because he feared whites would not migrate to an area where their own labor was devalued unfairly by the institution of black slavery. Periodically, Whitman expressed outrage at practices that furthered slavery itself: for example, he was incensed at laws that made possible the importation of slaves by way of Brazil. Like Lincoln, he consistently opposed slavery and its further extension, even while he knew (again like Lincoln) that the more extreme abolitionists threatened the Union itself. In a famous incident, Whitman lost his position as editor of the *Eagle* because the publisher, Isaac Van Anden, as an "Old Hunker" (a member of a political faction within the New York Democratic party that opposed anti-slavery agitation), sided with conservative pro-slavery Democrats. He could no longer abide Whitman's support of free soil and the Wilmot Proviso (a legislative proposal designed to stop the expansion of slavery into the western territories).

Fortunately, on February 9, 1848, Whitman met, between acts of a performance at the Broadway Theatre in New York, J. E. McClure, who intended to launch a New Orleans paper, the *Crescent*, with an associate, A. H. Hayes. In a stunningly short time – reportedly in 15 minutes – McClure struck a deal with Whitman to become editor and provided him with an advance to cover his travel expenses to New Orleans. Whitman's younger brother Jeff, then only 15 years old, decided to travel with Walt and work as an office boy on the paper. The journey – by train, steamboat, and stagecoach – widened Walt's sense of the country's scope and diversity, as he left the New York City and

Long Island area for the first time. Once in New Orleans, Walt did *not* have the famous New Orleans romance with a beautiful Creole woman, a relationship first imagined by the biographer Henry Bryan Binns and further elaborated by others who were charmed by the city's exoticism and eager to identify heterosexual desires in the poet. The published versions of his New Orleans poem called "Once I Pass'd Through a Populous City" seem to recount a romance with a woman, though the original manuscript reveals that he initially wrote with a male lover in mind. Here, as is so often the case, Whitman's manuscripts provide an insight into the original motivations and tonalities of his poems, often revealing aspects of his thoughts that his published versions erased or disguised.

Whatever the nature of his personal attachments in New Orleans, he certainly encountered a city full of color and excitement. He wandered the French quarter and the old French market, attracted by "the Indian and negro hucksters with their wares" and the "great Creole mulatto woman" who sold him the best coffee he ever tasted. He enjoyed the "splendid and roomy bars" (with "exquisite wines, and the perfect and mild French brandy") that were packed with soldiers who had recently returned from the war with Mexico, and it was in New Orleans that his first encounters with young men who had seen battle, many of them recovering from war wounds, occurred, a precursor of his Civil War experiences. He was entranced by the intoxicating mix of languages – French and Spanish and English – in that cosmopolitan city and began to see the possibilities of a distinctive American culture emerging from the melding of races and backgrounds (his own fondness for using French terms may well have derived from his New Orleans stay). But the exotic nature of the Southern city was not without its horrors: slaves were auctioned within an easy walk of where the Whitman brothers were lodging at the Tremont House, around the corner from Lafayette Square. Whitman never forgot the experience of seeing humans on the selling block, and he kept a notice of a slave auction hanging in his room for many years as a reminder that such dehumanizing events occurred regularly in the United States. The slave auction was an experience that he would later incorporate in his poem "I Sing the Body Electric."

Walt felt wonderfully healthy in New Orleans, concluding that it agreed with him better than New York, but Jeff was often sick with dysentery, and his illness and homesickness contributed to their growing desire to return home. The final decision, though, was taken out of the hands of the brothers, as the *Crescent* owners exhibited what Whitman called a "singular sort of coldness" toward their new editor. They probably feared that this Northern editor would embarrass them because of his unorthodox ideas, especially about slavery. Whitman's sojourn in New Orleans lasted only three months.

His trip South produced a few lively sketches of New Orleans life and at least one poem, "Sailing the Mississippi at Midnight," in which the steamboat journey becomes a symbolic journey of life:

> Vast and starless, the pall of heaven
>   Laps on the trailing pall below;
> And forward, forward, in solemn darkness,
>   As if to the sea of the lost we go. (*EPF*, 42)

Throughout much of the 1840s Whitman wrote conventional poems like this one, often echoing the poet and editor William Cullen Bryant, and, at times, Shelley and Keats. Bryant – and the eighteenth-century graveyard school of English poetry – probably had the most important impact on his sensibility, as can be seen in his pre-*Leaves of Grass* poems "Our Future Lot," "Ambition," "The Winding-Up," "The Love that is Hereafter," and "Death of the Nature-Lover." The poetry of these years is artificial in diction and didactic in purpose; Whitman rarely seems inspired or innovative. Instead, tired language, conventional forms, and predictable thoughts usually render the poems inert:

> O, beauteous is the earth! and fair
> The splendors of Creation are:
> Nature's green robe, the shining sky,
> The winds that through the tree-tops sigh,
>   All speak a bounteous God. (*EPF*, 8)

By the end of the decade, however, Whitman had undertaken serious self-education in the art of poetry, conducted in a typically unorthodox way – he clipped essays and reviews about leading British and American writers, and as he studied them he began to be a more aggressive reader and a more resistant respondent. His marginalia on these articles demonstrate that he was now committed to write not in the manner of his predecessors but against them.

On July 16, 1849, the publisher, health guru, and social reformer Lorenzo Fowler confirmed Whitman's growing sense of personal capacity when his phrenological analysis of the poet's head led to a flattering – and in some ways quite accurate – description of his character. Whitman at this time believed strongly in phrenology, the reading of the "bumps" on the skull to determine which emotions and qualities were well developed and which needed further work. Fowler was a well-known manipulator of skulls, and often gave examinations and wrote out his "charts of bumps" in his New York office. On this particular day, he registered his new client as "W. Whitman (Age 29 Occupation Printer)" (Stern 1971, 102). As Fowler felt around the bumps and indentations of Whitman's head, he expressed some amazement at this printer's "large sized brain" and noted how "few men have *all* the social feelings as strong as you have." While Fowler's emphasis on how much Whitman loved home life and how much he wanted to become a husband and father and how he might make a good accountant seems wide of the mark, his other perceptions are keen:

> You choose to fight with tongue and pen rather than with your fist . . . You are in fact most *too* open at times and have not alway[s] enough restraint in speech . . . Your sense of justice, of right and wrong is strong and you can see much that is unjust and inhuman in the present condition of society. You are but little inclined to the spiritual or devotional and have but little regard for creeds or ceremonies . . . You have a good command of language especially if excited. (Stern 1971, 103–4)

It's as if Fowler's phrenological reading gave Whitman certification as a kind of ideal person, large in appetites and yet balanced in temperament, someone with what Fowler called a "grand physical constitution" (Stern 1971, 105) and therefore fit to become America's poet. In addition to bolstering Whitman's confidence, the positive reading of the "bumps" on his skull gave him some key vocabulary for *Leaves of Grass*. "Amativeness" and "adhesiveness," phrenological terms delineating affections between and among the sexes, were particularly important for him, and "adhesiveness" – the bonding of people of the same sex – provided Whitman with an early word for male–male affection at a time when such terms were not easy to find.

Whitman's association with Lorenzo Fowler and his brother Orson would prove to be of continuing importance well into the 1850s. The Fowler brothers, along with their brother-in-law Samuel R. Wells, ran the firm of Fowler and Wells, which would distribute the first edition of *Leaves of Grass*, publish the second anonymously, and provide a venue in their firm's magazine for one of Whitman's first self-reviews of his book. Whitman would later work for Fowler and Wells as a bookseller and as a writer for their *Life Illustrated* magazine. While he eventually drifted apart from them, the impact of phrenology always stayed with him: late in his life, Whitman admitted that "I probably have not got by the phrenology stage yet" (*WWC*, 1:385). When he later wrote in "Song of Myself" that "my palms cover continents" (*LG*, 61), he was still imagining himself as a kind of cosmic phrenologist, reading the mountains and valleys of continents to determine their telltale characteristics just as Fowler read the nooks and crannies of skulls. Whitman entered Fowler's studio as a "printer," but he left dreaming of larger ambitions.

Along with Fowler's 1849 description of Whitman as a "printer," we have other evidence about just how Whitman's career was perceived in 1850. James J. Brenton, owner of the *Long Island Democrat*, a newspaper on which Whitman had worked, put together a book in 1850 that collected what he called "sketches, essays, and poems by practical printers." The idea was to demonstrate that printers – "they who have so often assisted in ushering into the world the productions of others" – could also be writers, could "now in turn venture to originate ideas of their own, and appear before the public in the ambitious character of Authors" (Brenton, iii). The result, *Voices from the Press*, contained Whitman's short story "The Tomb Blossoms," the first appearance by Whitman in a book. He is presented as one of the printers who could also write, and in the contributors' notes we find a short biography of Whitman that describes him as a printer, former schoolteacher, and writer of popular sketches; he is now, we are told, "connected to the press" and is "an ardent politician of the radical democratic school." He is seen, in short, as anything but a poet: even his numerous early poems, many of which had appeared in Brenton's newspaper, are not mentioned. In 1850, only five years before publishing *Leaves of Grass*, a book that would forever change American literature, Whitman was still very much seen as just a "practical printer," but a huge transformation was just around the corner.

CHAPTER 2

"Many Manuscript Doings and Undoings": The Road toward *Leaves of Grass*

There has always been a mystery about Whitman at the end of the 1840s and through the early 1850s. Many critics and biographers have tried, but no one has fully explained the speed of his transformation from a newspaperman and "practical printer," and an unoriginal, conventional, and occasional poet, into the author of *Leaves of Grass*, a radical writer who abruptly abandoned conventional rhyme and meter and, in jottings begun at this time, exploited the odd loveliness of homely imagery, finding beauty in the commonplace but expressing it in an uncommon way, and, once he started, expressing it prolifically. One of the best places to search for the answer to that mystery is in Whitman's manuscript writings from this period. What is known as Whitman's earliest notebook (called "albot Wilson" in the *Notebooks and Unpublished Prose Manuscripts*) was long thought to date from 1847 but is now understood to be from about 1854. This extraordinary document contains early articulations of some of Whitman's most compelling ideas. Famous passages on "Dilation," on "True noble expanding American character," and on the "soul enfolding orbs" are memorable prose statements that express the newly expansive sense of self that Whitman was discovering, and we find him here creating the conditions – setting the tone and articulating the ideas – that would allow for the writing of *Leaves of Grass*. Late in his life, Whitman looked at this notebook and called it the "ABC" of *Leaves*, the very primer for the whole book.

A pivotal and empowering change came over Whitman at this time of poetic transformation. His politics – and especially his racial attitudes – underwent a profound alteration. As we have noted, Whitman the journalist spoke to the interests of the day and from a particular class perspective when he advanced the interests of white working men while seeming, at times, unconcerned about the plight of blacks. Perhaps the New Orleans experience had prompted a change in attitude, a change that was intensified by an increasing number of friendships with radical thinkers and writers who led Whitman to rethink his attitudes toward the issue of race. Whatever the cause, in Whitman's future-oriented poetry blacks become central to his new literary project and central to his understanding of democracy. Notebook passages assert that the poet has the "divine grammar of all tongues, and says indifferently and alike How are you friend? to the President in the midst of his cabinet, and Good day my brother, to Sambo, among the hoes of the sugar field" (*NUPM*, 1:61).

It appears that Whitman's increasing frustration with the Democratic party's compromising approaches to the slavery crisis led him to continue his political efforts through the more subtle and indirect means of experimental poetry, a poetry that he hoped would be read by masses of average Americans and would transform their way of thinking. In any event, his first notebook lines in the manner of *Leaves of Grass* focus directly on the fundamental issue dividing the United States. His notebook breaks into free verse for the first time in lines that seek to bind opposed categories, to link black and white, to join master and slave:

> I am the poet of slaves and of the masters of slaves
> . . .
> I am the poet of the body
> And I am the poet of the soul
> I go with the slaves of the earth equally with the masters
> And I will stand between the masters and the slaves,
> Entering into both so that both shall understand me alike. (*NUPM*,
>   1:67)

The audacity of that final line remains striking. While most people were lining up on one side or another, Whitman placed himself in that space – sometimes violent, sometimes sexual, always volatile – *between* master and slave. His extreme political despair led him to replace what he now named the "scum" of corrupt American politics in the 1850s with his own persona – a shaman, a culture-healer, an all-encompassing "I."

The new all-encompassing "I" that emerged in Whitman's early notebook became the main character of *Leaves of Grass*, the explosive book of 12 poems that he wrote in the early years of the 1850s, and for which he set some of the type, designed the cover, and carefully oversaw all the details. When Whitman wrote "I, now thirty-six years old, in perfect health, begin," he announced a new identity for himself, and his novitiate came at an age quite advanced for a poet. Keats had died ten years younger; Byron had died at exactly that age; Wordsworth and Coleridge produced *Lyrical Ballads* while both were in their twenties; Bryant had written "Thanatopsis," his best-known poem, at age 16; and most other great Romantic poets Whitman admired had done their most memorable work early in their adult lives. Whitman, in contrast, by the time he had reached his mid-thirties, seemed destined, if he were to achieve fame in any field, to do so as a journalist or perhaps as a writer of fiction, but no one could have guessed that this middle-aged writer of sensationalistic fiction and sentimental verse would suddenly begin to produce work that would eventually lead many to view him as America's greatest and most revolutionary poet.

One source of Whitman's influence was his radical reconception of the art of poetry. What we now think of as his "poetry" is actually a new kind of writing, a hybrid form that draws not only on the tones and diction of the Bible and on the traditions of British, European, and American literature, but equally on such things as American newspapers, booming mid-nineteenth-century political oratory, and the lingoes of the emerging urban working classes (of which he was a product and a member). Whitman immersed himself in American culture, and his work resonates through the multiple levels of that culture. It is a writing that reaches deep into the numerous corners of the roiling nineteenth-century society, absorbing the nation's stormy politics, its motley musical and theatrical stages, its athletic contests, and its new technologies (including the chemical art of photography and the rapidly developing printing trade). It is writing remarkably open to the century's scientific discoveries (evolutionary, geological, astronomical, archeological, and phrenological), to new discourses about

Figure 1 Daguerreotype portrait of Whitman (1854), called by Whitman's disciple R. M. Bucke "the Christ likeness." Ed Folsom collection.

the body (medical and sexual), and to advances in understandings about language (lexicographical, etymological, and theoretical).

"Births have brought us richness and variety," Whitman wrote in "Song of Myself," "And other births will bring us richness and variety" (*LG*, 80). Whitman's own family taught him that lesson, but it was a lesson he sought to learn again and again in all aspects of his life. He celebrated the self, but not a self that was narrowly and securely defined – rather a self that took the risks of imaginative absorption and creative dispersion. The opening words of the first poem in *Leaves of Grass*, the poem that would become "Song of Myself," set the tone for the book – pride in a nondiscriminating self mixed with a demand that the reader agree to give up, at least for the duration of the poem, biases and tenets and, instead, join the "I" on a dizzying journey of discovery: "I celebrate myself, / And what I assume you shall assume, / For every atom belonging to me as good belongs to you" (*LG 1855*, 13). "We are powerful and tremendous in ourselves," he wrote, but the power came in one's ability to open the self to its latent pluralities: "we are sufficient in the variety of ourselves" (*LG*, 341). Whitman's goal was the multitudinous self, a self capacious enough to identify with the vast variety of human types that American democracy was producing: he loved America's "loose drift of character, the inkling through random types" (*LG*, 186), and Whitman's pun on "ink" and "type" here would become his great metonymic invention – to turn human types into printed type, to ink character on a page, to turn a book into a man. "Camerado, this is no book," he writes, "Who touches this touches a man" (*LG*, 505), and throughout *Leaves*, we can feel an identity straining to make human contact through the print and paper: "I pass so poorly with paper and types . . . . I must pass with the contact of bodies and souls" (*LG 1855*, 57).

This extraordinary conflation of book and identity grew out of Whitman's experience as a printer and a newspaper editor. He was always conscious of the way that different types and different page sizes and different titles altered otherwise identical words: for him, paper and type were more than a vehicle to present poems, they were indeed bodies themselves. He conceived of the "body of his work" as something more than a dead metaphor. Thus he was always engaged in the act of bookmaking as well as poetry writing. He knew how to set type, and he knew how books were printed and bound. He wanted to have an actual physical involvement in the creation of the physical object of the book, and so he set a few pages of type for the first (1855) edition of *Leaves* and chose the large-paper format to give his long lines room to stretch across the page. Late in his life, Whitman noted how "I sometimes find myself more interested in book making than in book writing . . . the way books are made – that always excites my curiosity: the way books are written – that only attracts me once in a great while" (*WWC*, 4:233). He never stopped being a printer, and his various editions of *Leaves* all show the marks of his idiosyncratic printer's eye.

The mystery that has intrigued biographers and critics over the years has been about what prompted the transformation: did Whitman undergo some sort of spiritual illumination that opened the floodgates of a radical new kind of poetry, or was this poetry the result of an original and carefully calculated strategy to blend journalism, oratory, popular music, and other cultural forces into an innovative American voice like the one Ralph Waldo Emerson had called for in his essay "The Poet"? "Our logrolling, our stumps and their politics, our fisheries, our Negroes, and Indians, our boasts, and our repudiations, the wrath of rogues, and the pusillanimity of honest men, the northern trade, the southern planting, the western clearing, Oregon, and Texas, are yet unsung," wrote Emerson; "Yet America is a poem in our eyes; its ample geography dazzles the imagination, and it will not wait long for metres" (Emerson 1983, 465). Whitman began writing poetry that seemed, wildly yet systematically, to record every single thing that Emerson called for, and he began his preface to the 1855 *Leaves* by paraphrasing Emerson: "The United States themselves are essentially the greatest poem." The romantic view of Whitman is that he was suddenly inspired to impulsively write the poems that transformed American poetry; the more pragmatic view holds that he devoted himself in the five years before the first publication of *Leaves* to a disciplined series of experiments that led to the gradual and intricate structuring of his singular style. Was he truly the intoxicated poet Emerson imagined or was he the architect of a poetic persona that cleverly constructed itself according to Emerson's formula?

There is evidence to support both theories. We know very little about the details of Whitman's life in the early 1850s; it is as if he retreated from the public world to receive inspiration, and there are relatively few remaining manuscripts of the poems in the first edition of *Leaves*, leading many to believe that they emerged in a fury of inspiration. On the other hand, the manuscripts that do remain indicate that Whitman meticulously worked and reworked passages of his poems, heavily revising entire drafts of the poems, and that he issued detailed instructions to the Rome brothers, the printers who were setting his book in type, carefully overseeing every aspect of the production of his book.

The 1855 *Leaves of Grass*, as we have come to know it, consists of 12 poems, all either untitled or headed with the identical title "Leaves of Grass." But a manuscript now held at the Harry Ransom Center at the University of Texas indicates that Whitman referred to his 1855 poems by name, even though he would withhold the titles in print. In the manuscript, he gives most of the 12 poems first-line titles, a practice he would frequently employ during the rest of his career. Further, his listing of poems in the Texas manuscript appear in an order significantly different from the arrangement he finally settled on: "I celebrate myself" ("Song of Myself") came first (as it would in the printed edition), followed by "A young man came to me" (the poem that would develop into "Song of the Answerer"), "A child went forth" ("There Was a Child Went Forth"), "sauntering the pavement" ("Faces"), "great are the myths" ("Great Are the Myths"), "I wander all night" ("The Sleepers"), "Come closer to me" ("A Song for Occupations"), "Who learns my lesson complete" ("Who Learns My Lesson Complete"), "Clear the way there Jonathan" ("A Boston Ballad"), "Resurgemus" ("Europe: The 72d and 73d Years of These States"), "To think through the retrospections" ("To Think of Time"), and "Blacks" ("I Sing the Body Electric").

Whitman's use of these shorthand names allowed him to work out an arrangement of poems. Only one of the 12 poems had previously been published, and Whitman continued to call it by the same title under which it had originally appeared in the New York *Tribune* – "Resurgemus." Perhaps the most interesting working title is "Blacks" (the word is smudged almost beyond recognition on the manuscript), which underscores the fact that a slave auction is the setting of the poem that would become "I Sing the Body Electric." At the time he wrote these notes, "Blacks" was to be the concluding piece, a position that, had he published the poems in this order, would have intensified the importance of the slavery issue in the book. In two cases, Whitman groups pairs of poems: "A young man came to me" is bracketed with "A child went forth," and "Who learns my lesson

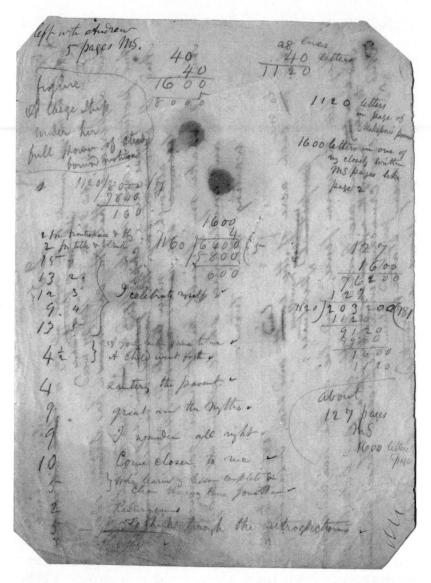

Figure 2 Whitman's alternative plan for structuring the 1855 edition of *Leaves of Grass*. Harry Ransom Humanities Research Center, University of Texas at Austin.

complete" is bracketed with and joined by an ampersand to "Clear the way there Jonathan." These subgroups suggest that Whitman had a hitherto unrecognized organizational plan for the book, one that involved small "clusters" of poems, a plan he would soon abandon in favor of what became the final arrangement.

Whitman seems, then, to have been both inspired poet and skilled craftsman, at once under the spell of his newly discovered and intoxicating free verse style while also remaining very much in control of it, adjusting and altering and rearranging. For the rest of his life, he would add, delete, fuse, separate, and rearrange poems as he issued six very distinct editions of *Leaves of Grass*. Emerson once described Whitman's poetry as "a remarkable mixture of the Bhagvat Ghita and the *New York Herald*" (Sanborn 2000, 144), and that odd joining of the scriptural and the vernacular, the transcendent and the mundane, effectively captures the quality of Whitman's work, work that most readers experience as simultaneously magical and commonplace, sublime and prosaic. It was work produced by a poet who was both sage and huckster, who touched the gods with ink-smudged fingers, and who was concerned as much with the sales and reviews of his book as with the state of the human soul.

It is striking that, 150 years after the appearance in 1855 of *Leaves of Grass*, we still know almost nothing for certain about its genesis. Long after published versions have appeared of all of Whitman's juvenilia, all of his late daybooks with listings of his supper guests and gas bills, all of his postcards and much of his marginalia, his poetry manuscripts have not been collected and edited, and few of them are readily accessible to students and scholars. When the variorum edition of *Leaves of Grass* was announced in 1955, the poetry manuscripts were promised as a central feature, but when the *Textual Variorum* (*LG Var.*) actually appeared in 1980, it contained only the published versions of each poem (in fact, only the published *book* versions – even the periodical variations have not yet been gathered and edited). There was speculation that a companion set of volumes dealing with the manuscripts would soon be following, but that has not happened, and Whitman's poetry manuscripts remain largely a mystery. Because so little is known about the manuscript origins of *Leaves*, we need to take some time to review just what we do know about the book's early composition and then examine a particularly revealing manuscript draft of a section of the long opening poem (eventually called "Song of Myself") of the 1855 edition. This will help us understand the intricate complexity of Whitman's process of revision.

Whitman kept a number of small notebooks in which some rough ideas and trial lines of some of the poems in the original *Leaves* can be found, and versions of those notebooks were included in Edward F. Grier's 1984 edition of Whitman's *Notebooks and Unpublished Prose Manuscripts*. But some of the early notebooks, including the one that contained the most important pre-*Leaves* notes, were lost when the Library of Congress packed them up and shipped them to a college in the midwestern United States for safekeeping during World War II; some are still missing, but several turned up unexpectedly in 1995. The so-called "earliest notebook," containing what are thought to be Whitman's first notes leading to *Leaves of Grass*, was one of the recovered items, and, while most of it had already been transcribed in *NUPM*, the physical notebook itself offers evidence of dating unavailable to Grier (who made his transcriptions from microfilm and photostats, which had been the only surviving evidence). These early notebooks – a number of which contain what could be considered preliminary versions of *Leaves* poems – have still not been fully examined and evaluated in relation to what they reveal about Whitman's writing process and what they tell us about the development of the 1855 *Leaves*.

Because of this lack of knowledge about Whitman's notebooks, critics and biographers have usually portrayed *Leaves* as an artistic immaculate conception, apparently emerging from nowhere. Most biographers, from John Burroughs and Richard Maurice Bucke in the nineteenth century on up to the most recent, have been remarkably vague about Whitman's actual writing of the original *Leaves*. Since Whitman directly contributed to both Burroughs's and Bucke's books, it is useful to recall just how they present the composition of the first *Leaves*. Burroughs, writing in 1867 and repeating phrases Whitman had given him, tells us the writing process was relatively brief and intense:

> It is at this period (1853 and the season immediately following,) that I come on the first inkling of *Leaves of Grass*. Walt Whitman is now thirty-four years old, and in the full fruition of health and physique . . . In 1855, then, after many manuscript doings and undoings, and much matter destroyed, and two or three complete re-writings, the essential foundation of *Leaves of Grass* was laid and the superstructure raised. (Burroughs 1867, 83)

Burroughs's words echo Whitman's own description that he included in a chronology of his life (he claims to have written this in 1856 or 1857, though he did not publish it until much later):

> '55 . . . Commenced putting *Leaves of Grass* to press for good, at the job printing office of my friends, the brothers Rome, in Brooklyn, after many MS. doings and undoings – (I had great trouble in leaving out the stock "poetical" touches, but succeeded at last.) (*PW*, 1:22; Traubel 1889, 4)

Bucke, in his biography, adds some specificity to this outline; Whitman tells us, or so Bucke says, that he

> had more or less consciously the plan of the poems in his mind for eight years before, and that during those eight years they took many shapes; that in the course of those years he wrote and destroyed a great deal; that, at the last, the work assumed a form very different from any at first expected; but that from first to last (from the first definite conception of the work in say 1853–'54, until its completion in 1881) his underlying purpose was *religious* . . . By the spring of 1855, Walt Whitman had found or made a style in which he could express himself, and in that style he had (after, as he has told me, elaborately building up the structure, and then utterly demolishing it, five different times) written twelve poems, and a long prose preface which was simply another poem. (Bucke 1883, 135, 137)

All subsequent descriptions of Whitman's compositional process derive from Bucke's and Burroughs's early descriptions, both of which were endorsed by (and largely written by) Whitman himself. The problem has been that those "MS. doings and undoings" and those "five different" versions of the book apparently disappeared, and scholars have been left guessing at whether what we have here is another of Whitman's infamous exaggerations or an actual description of invaluable but lost manuscript materials. If there were indeed five complete, different manuscript versions of *Leaves*, the evidence has never been found.

Whitman himself, late in his life, talked occasionally with his young friend Horace Traubel about the missing manuscripts of the first *Leaves of Grass*. In 1891 (in a conversation not published until 1996), Whitman reminisced about the early versions in a suggestive way:

Bucke probably does not know that long long ago, before the 'Leaves' had ever been to the printer, I had them in half a dozen forms – larger, smaller, recast, outcast, taken apart, put together – viewing them from every point I knew – even at the last not putting them together and out with any idea that they must eternally remain unchanged. (*WWC*, 8:351)

Here Whitman seems to suggest that he has been withholding evidence even from his good friend and loyal disciple Bucke (perhaps he has forgotten that Bucke already included in his biography the comment about five versions of the book), but here the form of those "MS. doings and undoings" seems even more fluid and fragmentary: "recast, outcast, taken apart, put together." Three versions, five versions, six versions: the actual number will never be known, and the nature of the "versions" can never be fully determined. All we finally can know, as Roger Asselineau observed in the 1950s, is that the evolution of the first *Leaves* "was a slow growth with many complex exchanges which we can guess at, but which it is impossible for lack of documentation to follow in detail or completely reconstruct. Only the result of this evolution has reached us" (Asselineau 1960, 1962, 1:45).

Most biographies and critical studies finesse the issue of Whitman's process of writing the original *Leaves of Grass* by referring vaguely to the now-missing "manuscript" for the book. "The manuscript" comes to be for biographers a convenient term for an assumed final handwritten "printer's copy" of *Leaves*, and the term has some basis in Whitman's own descriptions. On a couple of occasions late in his life, he mentioned "the manuscript" to Traubel: "You have asked me questions about the manuscript of the first edition. It was burned. Rome [the printer] kept it several years, but one day, by accident, it got away from us entirely – was used to kindle the fire or to feed the rag man" (*WWC*, 1:92). Another time, Whitman recalled that "[t]he first manuscript copy of the Leaves – 1855 – the first edition – is gone – irretrievably lost – went to the ragman: . . . But I make nothing of that – of the money value of the manuscripts – attach no importance to curios" (*WWC*, 2:56). By the time he made those statements, however, he was struck by how copies of the first edition of *Leaves* had become collectors' items and were selling for high prices, and he had begun to realize how valuable the 1855 manuscript would have been had he kept it: "The collectors are inflamed with the curio desire but to me the appetite is unwholesome," he said, even as he went on to think of how the money he might earn from such "curios" would help him take care of his mentally incapacitated brother Eddy: "And yet, . . . for Eddy's sake it might be wise for me to husband such stuff" (*WWC*, 2:56).

It is difficult, on the basis of any biographical images of Whitman, to imagine him actually writing five or six complete drafts of *Leaves*. If we want to picture him in the act of writing and revising, in fact, we have very little evidence to go on. His brother George gives us one of the few contemporary reports of his early writing habits, and his recollection of Walt is hardly of the disciplined wordsmith: "He would lie abed late, and after getting up would write a few hours if he took the notion – perhaps would go off the rest of the day. We were all at work – all except Walt" (Traubel 1893, 35). Bucke, again aided by Whitman, offers a more active portrayal of the poet at work: "Early in 1855 he was writing *Leaves of Grass* from time to time, getting it in shape. Wrote at the opera, in the street, on the ferry-boat, at the sea-side, in the fields, sometimes stopped work to write. Certainly no book was ever more directly written from living impulses and impromptu sights, and less in the abstract" (Bucke 1883, 25–6).

Whitman, throughout his whole life, would try to keep alive this active, experimental image of his younger self, combining it – sometimes uneasily – with his claim of meticulous revision. An anonymous London, Ontario, interviewer in 1880, for example, reported that Whitman said he "gave this work [*Leaves*] a great deal of revision, experiencing a difficulty in eliminating the stock poetical touches, if the idea may be conveyed in that way" (Myerson 1991, 20). To the end of his life, Whitman would continue to extol the virtues of ceaseless revision:

> I know an author's temptation always to [revise] – I myself, for one – I am always tempted to put in, take out, change. Though, having been a printer myself, I have what may be called an anticipatory eye – know pretty well as I write how a thing will turn up in the type – appear – take form. But in spite of that, I remember how, years ago, I used to wish for the privilege for myself – the privilege to alter – even extensively. (*WWC*, 5:390)

It was important, in other words, for Whitman to portray himself both as the casual outdoor writer, jotting things down spontaneously while crossing Brooklyn Ferry, and as the careful craftsman, continually worrying over insertions and deletions, searching always for the precise word. His manuscripts demonstrate that he was in fact *both* kinds of writer; there are signs of speed and spontaneity in his notebooks and brief jottings, but also, in his more extended manuscripts, signs of careful, nearly obsessive, revising.

There is, however, more evidence of the process than we have up to this point assumed. All the extant manuscripts of the poems in the first edition of *Leaves* are now being gathered for inclusion in the online *Walt Whitman Archive* (www.whitmanarchive.org). This process of gathering has revealed some fascinating traces of Whitman's manuscript doings and undoings. In addition to the notebooks that have been known for nearly a century, there also exist a large number of manuscript fragments on various single sheets and scraps of paper, containing lines and passages very close to those that appear in the 1855 *Leaves*. These fragments do indicate different stages of composition and revision, and most clearly date from later than the notebooks, which contain much rougher notes toward the book.

We mentioned earlier the manuscript preserved in the University of Texas Humanities Research Center, the one on which Whitman listed and named the poems for the 1855 edition of *Leaves*. This manuscript provides the first actual evidence of the extent of his active involvement in the design and structuring of the 1855 *Leaves* and allows us finally to confirm some previously unsubstantiated claims about the first edition – including his recollection that his prose preface to the first *Leaves* was added at the last minute ("It was written hastily while the first edition was being printed in 1855" [*Corr.*, 2:100]). The Texas manuscript – worn and soiled, after obviously spending some time on the Rome brothers' printing-shop floor – consists of, on one side (see figure 3 below), a heavily revised section of a proto-version of the poem that would eventually become "Song of Myself" (key images of the eventual poem here appear in surprising juxtapositions); on the other side (see figure 2 above) are Whitman's scribbled notes for the arrangement, size, and decoration of the 1855 *Leaves*. We have already talked about the side of the manuscript on which Whitman made his list of poems; let's focus now on the other side – the weird proto-version of a section of "Song of Myself."

Whitman often wrote notes and drafts on the backs of various documents, including the backs of abandoned drafts of poems, and that is the case with this manuscript. But what is striking here is that the abandoned poetry on the verso appears to be a section of an entirely different version of "Song of Myself" from the one Whitman published. It may be the only remaining evidence that there once actually was an entirely different version of the 1855 *Leaves*. Let's take a close look at this draft fragment. Here is a transcription of the poetry side of the manuscript:

25

*tr (And to me each minute of the night and day is ~~chock with something~~ vital and visible as

~~vital live as flesh is~~

trs in here page 34 – And I say the stars are not echoes
And I perceive that the ~~salt marsh~~ sedgy weed has ~~delicious~~ refreshing odors;
And potatoes and milk afford a ~~fit breakfast~~ dinner of state,
And I ~~dare not say~~ guess the ~~the bay mare is less than I mocking bird~~ chipping bird sings as well as I,
~~because~~ although she ~~reads no newspaper;~~ never learned the gamut;
And to shake my friendly right hand governors
and millionaires shall stand all day,
waiting their turns.

And ~~on~~ to me each acre of the ~~earth~~ land and sea, ~~I behold~~ exhibits ~~to me~~
~~perpetual~~ ~~unending~~ ∧marvellous pictures;
They ~~fill~~ the worm-fence, and lie on the heaped stones
and are hooked to the elder and poke-weed
~~And to me each~~ every ~~minute of the night and day is filled with a [illegible] joy.~~
And ∧to me the cow crunching with depressed head ~~surpasses~~ is an a ~~every~~ statue ∧perfect and plumb.
[illegible line, cut off]

This manuscript passage, it turns out, is made up of versions of lines from numerous places widely scattered in the first published version of the poem (and of the 1855 preface). From this one passage, in fact, lines scatter throughout what would become the printed version of "Song of Myself," and pieces reappear in what eventually would be sections 5, 13, 16, 31, 36, and 43, while other pieces appear in the poem eventually entitled "To Think of Time" and the pre-1855 manuscript poem "Pictures."

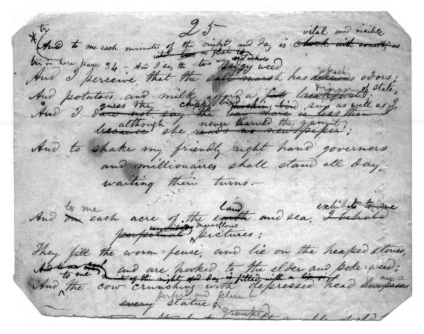

Figure 3 Draft lines from "Song of Myself." Harry Ransom Humanities Research Center, University of Texas at Austin.

Virtually every line of this early version of a section of "Song of Myself," then, gets used somewhere in the poem or elsewhere in *Leaves*. But the section itself is entirely dismantled and scattered; it ceases to exist as a unit. We recall Whitman's comment that his early drafts of *Leaves* were "recast, outcast, taken apart, put together." It's as if he mined early drafts for lines much like some sort of proto-word-processing system, lifting and moving lines and juxtaposing them with others, dissolving entire sections into other newly forming sections. This evidence strongly suggests that for Whitman the line was the basic unit of his poetry, since he seems always to move entire lines. This habit of composition may well have derived from Whitman's experience as a typesetter, where lines of text were separate, moveable units assembled into galleys. For Whitman, then, passages emerge from the juxtaposition and accretion of lines, and those lines can be recast and put together in different combinations to form different but equally coherent larger units.

These notes were written quite close to the publication of *Leaves*, and so this manuscript reveals that Whitman was actively making substantive last-minute changes – reorganizing, adding, and deleting, even while Andrew Rome was typesetting the poetry. These manuscripts suggest that the poems of the 1855 *Leaves of Grass* were extremely unstable right up to their being set in type (and even after that, since we now know that Whitman stopped the press at least once to rewrite a line and another time to correct a typographical error in the preface).

Many biographers have assumed – since the "earliest" notebook to contain lines that sound like precursors to the 1855 *Leaves* had been mistakenly dated 1847 – that Whitman must have been working for nearly ten years on drafts and trials of the poems that would appear in *Leaves*. But Esther Shephard argued in the 1950s that the evidence for the 1847 dating was faulty. Now that the notebook has been recovered by the Library of Congress and is available for examination on the World Wide Web, it is clear that Whitman, in characteristic fashion, cut out already used pages from an earlier notebook and used the blank pages and almost-blank pages as a new notebook sometime around 1854. All of this is to say that he moved from first jottings to final product in a much briefer period than is usually thought. If he in fact composed three or four or five or six separate drafts of the 1855 *Leaves*, he did so with astonishing speed. The available evidence would seem to indicate that the first edition of *Leaves* was no more than two years, and perhaps significantly less, in the making – from notebook jottings to printed book.

The Texas manuscript, with the proto-version on one side and the printer's instructions on the other, gives us a snapshot of how quickly the poem was coming together, since, as we noted earlier, the apparently abandoned version of the poem on the verso of the sheet contains a number 25 on it, indicating that it is part of a longer manuscript. (It also contains the intriguing note "tr[an]s[fer] in here page 34," indicating that Whitman was in fact doing a lot of "taking apart and putting together," pre-computer cutting and pasting that, if this one example is an accurate indication of his general process, was breathtaking in the complexity and scope of rearrangement.) It is a process that invites us to play the dangerous but instructive game of shuffling Whitman's lines all through "Song of Myself" (or, indeed, all through the 1855 *Leaves*) and discovering how easily new poems emerge that sound perfectly plausible: Whitman's lines, all concerned with absorption and the celebration of the democratic scatter of the world, are often interchangeable, and, when shuffled in myriad ways, keep forming different poems that say the same things.

Let's look closely now at the last line from this manuscript proto-version of the poem that would become "Song of Myself": "And ^to me the cow crunching with depressed head ~~surpasses~~ is ~~an~~ a ~~every~~ statue ^perfect and plumb." It is one of the stranger lines in Whitman's poetry, but it offers a key to one of the central meanings of his work. On one hand, it is a simple and typical Whitmanian statement that common natural life outshines art. But the oddness of the word "crunching" and the surprising juxtaposition of a grazing cow and a statue captures something we recognize as Whitman's idiosyncratic genius. In the context of the manuscript passage, the image is the culminating emblem of an emphasis on the artistic importance of the diurnal, the small, the neglected, the commonplace. The first line, insisting on how each minute is "vital and visible," evokes sight, and then Whitman systematically engages each of the senses: the second line (with the "echoes") suggests hearing, the third line (with the "refreshing odors") smell, the fourth (with "potatoes and milk") taste, the fifth (with the singing bird) sound again, and the sixth (with the shaking hands) touch. Then the passage turns the world into an infinite art gallery, where every sensation becomes a work of art worthy of display: "And ~~on~~ to me each acre of the ~~earth~~ land and sea, ~~I behold~~ exhibits ~~to me perpetual~~ ^unending marvellous pictures." Whitman then populates every remote crevice of the world with these exhibits – the worm-fence (a kind of zigzag fence), the heaped stones, and the weeds (in an image that would later appear in section 5 of "Song," where it would be the extreme border of "love," "the kelson of creation") – and, by offering us the image of the crunching cow as a perfect statue, he clinches his argument about the teeming art gallery that is available to us every minute of the day through every sensation.

When the line appears in the published version of the poem, it comes near the end of a slightly different kind of catalog, one that begins with "I believe a leaf of grass is no less than the journey-work of the stars" and goes on to juxtapose small and large, the tiny and the vast, the commonplace and the exalted: we get pismires, grains of sand, wren-eggs, tree-toads, and blackberries offered as "a chef-d'ouvre for the highest," fit to "adorn the parlors of heaven," before the culminating series:

> And the narrowest hinge in my hand puts to scorn all machinery,
> And the cow crunching with depressed head surpasses any statue,
> And a mouse is miracle enough to stagger sextillions of infidels,
> And I could come every afternoon of my life to look at the farmer's girl
> boiling her iron tea-kettle and baking shortcake. (*LG 1855*, 34)

In this new context, the image is more incongruous. The cow seems too large in this catalog of the small (blackberries, wrens' eggs, knuckle joints, mice, and a *cow*?), and its comparison to a statue is not parallel to the other comparisons, which are all based on differentials in size and number and complexity (journeywork of stars, parlors of heaven, all machinery, sextillions of infidels, and *any statue*?). While, in the catalog of Whitman's poem, the image may be harmlessly absorbed into the cascade of his images, once we have seen the manuscript where the line is more precisely situated among analogous images, we begin to realize that the line in its new context is somewhat out of place, as if Whitman had moved it randomly.

So why would Whitman have made this decision? Surely the final version of the first *Leaves* did not result from a random shuffling of lines. To begin to answer why it finally appears where it does, we need to track the line back through even earlier layers of Whitman's manuscript "doings and undoings." In Whitman's recovered "earliest" notebook (Library of Congress Notebook #80), the notebook we mentioned earlier and the one generally thought to contain the first stirrings of "Song of Myself," there is a two-page passage in which the "cow crunching" line reappears, this time in the context of a catalog demonstrating that Whitman is "the poet of little things." But if this notebook version is in fact the earliest of Whitman's manuscript drafts, the lines here are surprisingly much closer to the arrangement Whitman ended up with in the first edition of *Leaves*.

Is this notebook draft, then, actually a *later* revision of the apparently extensive draft of the proto-"Song" evidenced in the Texas manuscript passage we have been examining, or did Whitman distribute the images in this notebook into an extensive draft of the poem that he later abandoned, after which he returned to his early notes to write his final draft? The more we investigate the evidence, the more confusing

Whitman's process of revision seems. Here is the relevant passage from the notebook:

> I am the poet of little things and of babes
> Of each gnat in the air, and of beetles rolling balls of dung,
> Afar in the sky was a nest
> And my soul flew thither, and squat, and looked out,
> And saw the journeywork of suns and systems of suns,
> And that a leaf of grass is not less than they
> And that the pismire is equally perfect, and all grains of sand, and every
>   egg of the wren.
> And the tree-toad is a chef' d ouvre for the highest.
> And the running-blackberry would adorn the parlors of Heaven
> And the cow crunching with depressed neck surpasses every statue,
> And pictures great and small crowd the rail-fence, and hang on its
>   heaped stones and elder and poke-weed.
> *I am the poet of Equality*
>
> And a mouse is miracle enough to stagger trillions of infidels.
> And I cannot put my toe anywhere to the ground
> But it must touch numberless and curious books
> Each one scorning all that schools and science can do fully to translate
>   them
>
> And the salt marsh and creek have delicious odors,
> And potato and ears of maize make a fat breakfast,
> And huckleberrys from the woods distill joyous deliriums. (*NUPM*,
>   1:70–2)

This notebook passage has elements of both the proto-"Song" passage and the published passage. Here the lines up through the crunching cow image are a near-draft of the published passage, and the lines following the crunching cow image are versions of lines that appear in the Texas draft fragment – from the fence, stones, and pokeweed through the odors of the salt marsh and on through the potatoes (here combined with maize for a "fat breakfast" instead of combined with milk for a "dinner of state"). The mouse–infidels image becomes part of the published passage, but some of the images just drop away, not to be used anywhere (like the huckleberry-induced "joyous deliriums"). In this notebook passage, the sequence of images seems to produce a key declaration – "*I am the poet of Equality*" – and all the lines support this claim in some way, with the poet equating the significance of little things to large things and discovering the power of the commonplace (from those powerful huckleberries to the statue-surpassing cows).

So, if we assume the notebook passage is the earliest one, then Whitman clearly broke up the passage and recombined the images in one of the drafts of *Leaves*, then moved the crunching-cow line back to the grouping it had originally been in. Even though, as we have noted, the line does not fit quite as well in the large/small grouping as it did in the nature-better-than-art grouping, there are good formal and thematic reasons Whitman may have chosen to move it there. First, the sequence of lines in the 1855 *Leaves* begins with the central assertion of Whitman's book, its title trope: "I believe a leaf of grass is no less than the journeywork of the stars." Nearly twenty pages after the unnamed child had asked "What is the grass?" (*LG 1855*, 16), the question that in many ways precipitates the rest of the long poem, the poet is still answering it, and the "cow crunching with depressed head" carries on the answer, for the cow of course is eating grass.

Let us consider for a moment some of the wider implications of the crunching cow image. As George Hutchinson argues, the "riddle of the grass" is the central mystery that Whitman deals with in the first edition of *Leaves*:

> The riddle of the grass and the riddle of death are fully entwined in Whitman's conception, binding all the other riddles of "Song of Myself" together . . . To get to the bottom of the riddle of the grass is to get to the bottom of death and democracy, and to be renewed with supreme power. The dead are absorbed into the earth, their bodies broken apart to feed the grass, which in turn feeds us – as Whitman would feed us after he departs at the open end of his poem, "and filter and fibre [our] blood." Thus "the smallest sprout shows there is really no death, / And if ever there was it led forward life." The way in which Whitman leads us toward a solution of the riddle of the grass by enacting its germination (and, metaphorically, his own) is the process of the poem. (Hutchinson 1986, 75)

Thus, suggests Hutchinson, the image of the cow eating grass is at the center of the riddle-structure of the poem: "'How is it I extract strength from the beef I eat?' (answer: because the cattle eat grass, which grows from soil well-manured by death. Notice that this hidden 'answer' only implies an endless succession of further insoluble questions unfolding from the symbolism of grass)" (Hutchinson 1986, 80). The cow is one intermediary between the grass and us and the stars: in Whitman's composting faith, all the atoms of the universe cycle through various forms, and humans and the grass are literally stardust. The cow crunching the grass is an emblem and manifestation of the transformative and democratic energy of the universe, as all forms become all other forms.

Whitman always remained fascinated with this image of the cow crunching the grass, and throughout his life he invoked it, in a variety of contexts, from reveries about rural life to harangues about American politics. In *Memoranda During the War*, his book of Civil War memories, he uses the image to emphasize the ways that all profundities are devoured and digested by time:

> Let us not be deceiv'd by flatulent fleeting notorieties, political, official, literary and other. In any profound, philosophical consideration of our politics, literature &c., the best-known leaders – even the Presidents, Congresses, Governors, &c. – are only so many passing spears or patches of grass on which the cow feeds. (*PW*, 1:327)

In *Specimen Days*, when Whitman portrays himself sitting out in restorative nature, the crunching cow is never far from his sight and hearing and smell: "Near me are the cattle, feeding on corn-stalks. Occasionally a cow or the young bull . . . scratches and munches the far end of the log on which I sit. The fresh milky odor is quite perceptible" (*PW*, 1:159). Even late in his life, he was still obsessed with this image that had been with him from the very inception of *Leaves*: talking to Horace Traubel in 1890 about his book, Whitman made this remarkable statement:

> Leaves of Grass is an iconoclasm, it starts out to shatter the idols of porcelain worshipped by the average poets of our age – not ruthlessly – not wantonly – but to do it seriously, as having a great purpose imposed. I love to go along through the land, taking in all natural objects, events, – noting them. For instance, watching the cow crunching the grass – I can hear its melodious crunch – crunch – its bovine music: the lips, soul, of song as much there as anywhere. And the mother at home knitting her children's stockings: not forgetting the yarn – not omitting the needle. The poet would not have that – it would lack in sound,

elegance, what he calls poetic evidence. But for me it is my necessity –
it is all music – the *clef* of things – to discriminate – not so much to
produce an effect, or that at all – but to state the case – the case of the
universe: to seize upon its typical phasings. (*WWC*, 6:343)

Traubel notes that Whitman spoke these words with particular emotion: "This was all said with a great vehemence as if it came of deep
and long rumination." It is as if, for Whitman, this odd image of the
crunching cow gets at the very core of the meaning and music of
Leaves of Grass. Here, nearly forty years after starting *Leaves*, Whitman
recreates in his conversation with Traubel that passage from the first
"Song of Myself" where the "cow crunching" is followed by an expression of the love of the sounds of the domestic and the day-to-day: in
the first *Leaves* it was "And I could come every afternoon of my life
to look at the farmer's girl boiling her iron tea-kettle and baking
shortcake," and in 1890 it was "the mother at home knitting her
children's stockings."

We gain a sense of Whitman writing – actually *writing* – by tracing
the movement of this line about crunching cows from its first appearance in a notebook through a draft of *Leaves* and finally into the
printed version, where the line is folded into a section that immediately
precedes the astonishing image of Whitman as a kind of evolutionary
monument: "I find I incorporate gneiss and coal and long-threaded
moss and fruits and grains and esculent roots, / And am stucco'd with
quadrupeds and birds all over." Just as the crunching cow "surpasses
any statue," so does Whitman's body, which contains in its evolutionary
memory all the fruits and grains and roots and birds and quadrupeds
that he has just catalogued (the grass, the wren, the toad, the black-
berry, the mouse, the cow, the grain of the shortcake). And it is
significant that this section just precedes the section of "Song of Myself"
that begins "I think I could turn and live awhile with the animals . . .
they are so placid and self-contained, / I stand and look at them
sometimes half a day long." There was more than a randomness in
Whitman's scattering of his lines, though it is clear that many of our
favorite lines in the 1855 *Leaves* could easily and effectively appear
elsewhere in the book (and many of them apparently at some time *did*).

Whitman's drafts of the first *Leaves* reveal how central his "placid"
and lingering look at the animals really is. The process we have just
traced involving the image of the crunching cow is repeated many

times as Whitman constructs *Leaves of Grass*. Most of the early manuscripts are gone, but the ones that remain form the basis for an understanding of the compositional process of Whitman's book, an understanding that will remain rudimentary until all the extant manuscripts are gathered, sorted, and edited. Only then will we begin to comprehend the complexity of Whitman's drafting of the 1855 *Leaves*.

CHAPTER 3

"I Was Chilled with the Cold Types and Cylinder and Wet Paper Between Us": The First and Second Editions of *Leaves of Grass*

Whitman paid out of his own pocket for the production of the first edition of his book and had only 800 copies printed, 795 of which he bound at various times as his finances permitted. He designed the cover, chose the paper and binding, and set some of the type himself. He chose an oversize-format to allow for his long, absorptive poetic lines to flow across the page, making room for a poetry as spacious as the expanding American nation. Whitman believed that American poetry would have to be essentially different from any poetry written previously – it would have to look different, sound different, and deal with different subject matter if it was to guide the development of a radical new American democracy. So he designed his book to look unlike any previous book of poetry, and the binding was a key element of his innovation.

Whitman chose a dark-green ribbed morocco cloth to suggest the organic nature of the poetry, and his title set up a pun on "leaves" – the leaves (or pages) of this book would be like leaves of grass, hearty and alive, growing everywhere, a poetry of the outdoors, rooted in the soil of America. He designed the stamping on the cover: he gold-stamped the lush letters of "Leaves of Grass," with the very letters of the title sprouting roots and leaves, and he surrounded the title with images of foliage stamped into the morocco green, with even more foliage prominently gold-stamped on the spine. (When Whitman found enough money to bind another batch of the books, however, he made the binding a bit cheaper by leaving more of the stamped decorations ungilded, and he bound the last batch in paper wrappers.) It is a book whose stylized cover insists on an organic understanding of literature, with words rooted in nature, with language as abundant as grass. And just as striking as the fertile letters of his title are the letters that are missing on the cover – the letters of the author's name.

Though it was no secret who the author of *Leaves of Grass* was (Whitman's name did appear on the copyright notice on the back of the title page), the fact that he did not put his name on the title page was an unconventional and suggestive act (his name would in fact not appear on a title page of *Leaves* until the 1876 "Author's Edition" of the book, and then only when Whitman signed his name on the title page as each book was sold). The absence of a name indicated, perhaps, that the author of this book believed he spoke not for himself so much as for America. But opposite the title page was a portrait of Whitman, an engraving by Samuel Hollyer, based on a daguerreotype taken by the photographer Gabriel Harrison during the summer of 1854. It has become the most famous frontispiece in literary history, showing Walt in workman's clothes, shirt open, hat on and cocked to the side, standing insouciantly and fixing the reader with a challenging stare. It is a full-body pose that indicates Whitman's recalibration of the role of poet as the democratic spokesperson who no longer speaks only from the intellect and with the formality of tradition and education: the new poet pictured in Whitman's book is a poet who speaks from and with the whole body and who writes *outside*, in Nature, not in the library. It was what Whitman called "al fresco" poetry, poetry written outside the walls, the bounds, of convention and tradition.

Whitman's book was an extraordinary accomplishment: after trying for over a decade to address in journalism and fiction the social issues (such as education, temperance, slavery, prostitution, immigration, democratic representation) that challenged the new nation, Whitman now turned to an unprecedented form, a kind of experimental verse cast in unrhymed long lines with no identifiable meter, the voice an

Figure 4 Frontispiece portrait of Whitman from 1855 edition of *Leaves of Grass;* engraving by Samuel Hollyer. University of Iowa Special Collections.

uncanny combination of oratory, journalism, and the Bible – haranguing, mundane, and prophetic – all in the service of identifying a new American democratic attitude, an absorptive and accepting voice that would catalog the diversity of the country and manage to hold it all in a vast, single, unified identity. "Do I contradict myself?" he asked confidently toward the end of the long poem he would come to call "Song of Myself": "Very well then . . . . I contradict myself; / I am large . . . . I contain multitudes" (*LG 1855*, 55). This new voice spoke confidently of union at a time of incredible division and tension in the culture, and it spoke with the assurance of one for whom everything, no matter how degraded, could be celebrated as part of itself: "What is commonest and cheapest and nearest and easiest is Me." His work echoed with the lingo of the American urban working class and took pride in an American language that was forming as a tongue distinct from British English.

Whitman wrote this new poetry in free verse, picking up the rhythms of American speech and developing vast, flowing sentences that crossed over his lengthy lines, each one a kind of extended exhalation of breath. His poetry, he announced at the beginning of "Song of Myself," was based on "respiration and inspiration," the breathing in of the world around him in all its diversity and the breathing out again in words that echoed that world. For him, poetry was very much a physical activity, an exercise of the body:

> My respiration and inspiration . . . . the beating of my heart . . . . the
>   passing of blood and air through my lungs,
> The sniff of green leaves and dry leaves, and of the shore and darkcolored
>   sea-rocks, and of hay in the barn,
> The sound of the belched words of my voice . . . . words loosed to the
>   eddies of the wind. (*LG 1855*, 13)

Whitman reveled in slangy words like "sniff" and "belch," with their edge of earthiness and natural process: the idea of poetry as a kind of sniffing and belching upset traditionalists but excited others, who saw in Whitman's poetry something new, closer to the body, a poetry expressed out of a primitive urge rather than the result of studied procedure. The "belch'd words of my voice" were words that were not abstract and separate from the body, but rather words made by the body's blood and the body's breathing and the body's muscles.

Whitman emphasizes that words don't come into existence as print on paper; they begin in an actual process of the body. Without "the beating of my heart," the blood does not circulate to the brain and ideas don't form; and blood needs to circulate to the arms and hands so that ideas can get put on paper by the workings of muscles and bones. And words don't get pushed out of the mouth by their own power, either, but rather by the physiological functioning of "the passing of blood and air through my lungs." Whitman often works to reattach the act of writing and speaking poetry to the functioning of the body: "I believe in the flesh and the appetites, / Seeing hearing and feeling are miracles, and each part and tag of me is a miracle" (*LG 1855*, 29).

Whitman thus invents a style that captures the easy influx of sensory experience, that catalogs the world he sees, hears, smells, tastes, and touches. Throughout the first edition of *Leaves*, he pictures himself as the ultimate absorber of physical experience, with the five senses wide open, allowing each moment to redefine who and what he is: "In me the caresser of life wherever moving"; "I am of old and young, of the foolish as much as the wise"; "I resist anything better than my own diversity"; "To me the converging objects of the universe per-petually flow, / All are written to me, and I must get what the writing means" (*LG 1855*, 20, 23, 24, 26). The speaker of *Leaves* is someone whose senses are charged up, heightened, electric:

I have instant conductors all over me whether I pass or stop,
They seize every object and lead it harmlessly through me.

I merely stir, press, feel with my fingers, and am happy,
To touch my person to some one else's is about as much as I can stand.

Is this then a touch? . . . . quivering me to a new identity. (*LG 1855*, 32)

By simply moving the legs to carry the organs of sense through the world, Whitman suggests, any self can grow exponentially. The less we discriminate, the fewer things we refuse to absorb through our senses, the larger we become. And so Whitman's notorious catalogs, sometimes stretching for pages at a time, can be read as a series of random and endless democratic moments, incidents of sensory intake, each given its own line, and each generated simply by turning the head on the neck and apprehending the world. "My head evolves on my neck" (*LG 1855*, 46), Whitman writes, and the word "evolves" suggests both a revolving – a turning of the head to take in more of the world's sights and sounds and smells – and an "evolving," a growth and progression of the self that occurs when it accumulates additional experience: sees new vistas, hears new ideas, tastes the bounty of the world. Whitman later altered this line to "My head slues round on my neck" (*LG*, 76), and his change emphasizes the pivot of the head, the sweeping of the eyes, as the endless sensations of the world enter the body and remake the soul.

Part of Whitman's invention of a new democratic style involved his creation of the reader as a major character in his poems. "You" comes to play as vital a role as "I." Whitman loved the easy fluidity of the English second-person pronoun, which moved seamlessly from signaling an intimate encounter with a lover to indicating an address to the whole nation or the whole world. In English, unlike in most other languages, there is only one pronoun to refer to a single or plural other, someone you know well or someone you do not know at all: in English, a lover and a stranger are both "you," and a single person and a crowd are both "you." So when Whitman begins his first poem with "I celebrate myself, / And what I assume you shall assume, / For every atom belonging to me as good belongs to you" (*LG 1855*, 13), he addresses the reader at once as part of a vast readership, a world of possible "you"s, but he also addresses the reader as a single, separate, and important person, an intimate "you" to whom this "I" speaks in confidence: "This hour I tell things in confidence, / I might not tell everybody but I will tell you" (*LG 1855*, 25). We know that the things we are being told in confidence are in fact being told to everyone who reads this book, but the "you" does not seem impersonal and distant; rather, the "you" enfolds us in the poet's embrace and makes each of us a kind of co-creator of the poem.

Whitman thus turns the impersonal act of reading into an intimate experience and talks to us as if the print on the page were itself a sentient being, aware of our presence: "Listener up there! Here you . . . . what have you to confide to me? / Look in my face while I snuff the sidle of evening, / Talk honestly, for no one else hears you, and I stay only a minute longer" (*LG 1855*, 55). We as readers are being addressed more directly than we are used to being addressed by a writer, and we are even being asked to respond, to confide to the "I" of this poem our secrets, dreams, anxieties. Whitman's exclamation to the reader – "Listener up there!" – comes as a shock, because it expresses awareness of the physical positioning of the reader in relation to the text, the reader's face hovering above the page. When he instructs us to "look in my face," we recall the striking frontispiece wherein Whitman fixes us with his stare, and we might also hear a kind of printer's pun on "typeface": the "face" we are literally looking into at this moment of reading is the type on the page, the ink that Whitman is reminding us contains his words, his breath, his being.

The great twentieth-century Argentinian writer Jorge Luis Borges has written eloquently about how Whitman created in *Leaves of Grass* a singular fictional entity, a hero with a "threefold nature": one being Walt Whitman, the biographical entity living in the United States in the nineteenth century; the second being a projected shadow of that man, also named Walt Whitman, "magnified by hope, by joy, by exultation"; and, finally,

> also the reader, any reader, any one of his present or future readers. How this was done we shall never quite know. Whitman felt very keenly the strangeness of the link between the man who reads a book and the unknown or dead man who wrote it; this may have helped him to work the miracle he needed. He makes the reader speak to him: "What do you hear Walt Whitman?"

Whitman's great feat, Borges says, was to make "the editor of the Brooklyn *Daily Eagle* into Walt Whitman, into America, into all of us," and this "plan of making a character out of the writer and the reader," Borges claims, "has not been attempted again; and, for all we know, it may be impossible" (Jaén 1969, xv–xvii).

Borges captures here the revolutionary nature of Whitman's accomplishment. Whitman creates a "you" that is an intimate confidant and, at the same time, a vast democratic readership – everyone who can read is invited to this one-on-one personal encounter. He creates, in other words, a new democratic act of reading, where the author is not so much the "authority" as the companion, someone not only to be listened to but also to be talked to. Whitman always believed that a democracy would have to develop new, more rigorous reading habits, would have to learn to wrestle with authority and never passively accept what authority claimed. So democracy would require a new concept of "author" and "reader," a more intimate interaction between the "I" and the "you" of any text.

It will help us to better understand the first edition of *Leaves* and Whitman's new poetic style if we zero in on the composition of an especially haunting and accomplished poem, eventually known as "The Sleepers." This poem appeared under the recurring label "Leaves of Grass," the fourth of the 12 poems in the first edition. In the 1856 *Leaves*, Whitman entitled it "Night Poem," and then "Sleep-Chasings" in 1860 and 1867. In the 1871 edition of *Leaves*, Whitman gave it its final title, "The Sleepers." In the context of the first edition of *Leaves*, "The Sleepers" offers Whitman's new democratic "I" the chance to slip across many boundaries. The persona of this poem is the most fluid "I" in all of Whitman, crossing gender and race, penetrating walls, invading minds of people around the world.

Whitman plays on the way that sleep dissipates a sharp sense of self-identity. Sleep is a state in which we sense conscious control of our thoughts slipping away, where we experience the weird, sometimes frightening, and often liberating escapes from the more rational forms of our waking lives. Thoughts and images and scenes that we may repress in waking thought are released in the dreaming state of sleep; habitual dichotomies and patterns of discrimination break down as we imagine ourselves in situations that we may be embarrassed to admit when we remember our dreams upon awakening. Whitman expresses this embarrassment in the poem, evoking dream-scenes that most of us have experienced in some form – finding ourselves naked in public ("my clothes were stolen while I was abed, / Now I am thrust forth, where shall I run?"), dreaming of our own death ("A shroud I see – and I am the shroud. . . . I wrap a body and lie in the coffin"), experiencing ourselves as someone else ("I am the actor and the actress . . . . the voter . . the politician, / The emigrant and the exile . . the criminal that stood in the box"), released from the categories of gender and class that, in our waking lives, define us.

Sleep for Whitman, then, is a democratic condition. Throughout the first edition of *Leaves*, he seeks those experiences that cross the boundaries of class, gender, and race: all humans live in bodies and apprehend the world through the five senses and breathe the same air. His emphasis on the body and on sensuality grows out of his belief that such an appeal to physical experience breaks down hierarchies and discriminations among his readers. To represent those experiences that we all share is to create a democratic poetry, a poetry accessible to everyone, a poetry that invites all readers to assume the role of Whitman's "you." Sleep is another of those democratic experiences. Not only do we all sleep, we all know and have felt the "breakdown" of "sleep-chasings," the way that falling asleep gives us the experience of losing control, the ways that dreams allow us to undergo shape-shifting, to wander worlds beyond our own waking experiences. Sleep, Whitman indicates in this poem, allows us finally to move into deeper and deeper levels of common psychic territory, where we all descend at night to plumb the depths of human emotion.

Among the fragmented dreams and nightmares that Whitman records in this poem are three longer dreams, one following upon another, that break the opening quick-moving pace of the poem and offer sustained narratives. This fluctuation between fast-paced catalogs of imagery and more deliberate narrative interludes is a characteristic of all the poems in the 1855 *Leaves*. The first sustained narrative in "The Sleepers" is a memory of General George Washington after the battle of Brooklyn Heights during the Revolutionary War, as he meets with his officers following the battle and "encircles their necks with his arm and kisses them on the cheek, / He kisses lightly the wet cheeks one after another" (*LG 1855*, 74). This tender moment softens the image of Washington and shows him unashamedly exhibiting affection to his comrades, as if offering a sanction for physical expressions of male–male affection. This scene is followed by a memory of the poet's mother spending the day with an American Indian woman who has come by to cane chairs; again, we have a scene of same-sex affection as "My mother looked in delight and amazement at the stranger," and "The more she looked upon her she loved her, / Never before had she seen such wonderful beauty and purity" (*LG 1855*, 74). This scene intensifies Whitman's portrayal of affection by carrying it across racial lines, as the white mother experiences deep affection for the Indian woman.

The third scene, however, is shocking in the abrupt change of tone. Suddenly the poem is taken over by a black slave's expression of hatred for his white master, and, for the first time in American poetry, a white poet turns over the narration of a poem to a black character:

Now Lucifer was not dead . . . . or if he was I am his sorrowful terrible
  heir;
I have been wronged . . . . I am oppressed . . . . I hate him that oppresses
  me,
I will either destroy him, or he shall release me.

Damn him! How he does defile me,
How he informs against my brother and sister and takes pay for their
  blood,
How he laughs when I look down the bend after the steamboat that
  carries away my woman.

Now the vast dusk bulk that is the whale's bulk . . . . it seems mine,
Warily, sportsman! though I lie so sleepy and sluggish, my tap is death.
  (*LG 1855*, 74)

This powerful threat by a slave named after the rebellious angel Lucifer
was, in 1855, an explosive moment in *Leaves of Grass*. This was a time
when slave rebellions were still common in the South, and a time
when the fear of a massive slave uprising haunted slaveholding states.
This slave's anger at the injustice of the slavery system is likened to a
whale, whose black bulk is hidden beneath the water, but whose
strength and size, when inflamed, could quickly destroy the "sportsman" who blithely captains the boat that seems in command, until
the whale's fluke taps death.

This scene is one of the most powerful antislavery statements
Whitman ever wrote, and it has a long and illuminating pre-history
in his manuscripts, where we find a number of versions of the passage,
indicating that he was well aware of the significance of this scene and
worked it over and over again, seeking just the right resonance. In
the same early notebook in which he wrote his "I am the poet of
slaves" passage that we looked at in the last chapter, he also wrote a
striking curse, angry words that he would eventually put in the mouth
of Lucifer. It is important to remember that these pages come very
soon after Whitman decides to speak for both the slaves and the
masters of slaves.

I am a Curse:

Sharper than ~~wind~~ serpent's
  eyes or wind of the
  ice-fields!

O topple down ~~like~~ Curse!
   topple more heavy than
   death!
I am lurid with rage!

I invoke Revenge to assist
   me –
I

A ~~divine fa~~

Let fate pursue them
I do not know any horror
   that is dreadful enough
   for them –
What is the worst whip
   you have

May the ~~genitals~~ that
   begat them rot
May the womb that begat

I will not listen
I will not spare

They shall ^not hide themselves
   in their graves
I will pursue them thither
Out with their [~~illegible~~] coffins –
Out with them from their
   shrouds!

The lappets of God shall
   not protect them

   ——————————

This shall be placed in the
   library of the laws,
And they shall be placed in
   the childs – doctors
     – songwriters

In a later draft, now at the University of Virginia, Whitman develops this curse and begins to more explicitly put it in the mouth of a slave:

> I am ~~black~~ a curse: a ~~black slave~~ negro ~~spoke~~ ~~felt thought~~ thinks me
> You ~~Youlle~~ cannot speak for ~~your~~him self, ~~slave,~~ negro – I lend ~~you~~ him
> my own ~~mouth~~ tongue
> ~~A black~~ {illegible} I ~~darted~~ like a snake from {his[?]} {your[?]} ^mouth. –
> ~~I~~ My eyes are bloodshot, they look down the river,
> A steamboat ~~carries off~~ paddles away my woman and children. –
> [previous two lines cancelled]
> ~~Around my neck I am~~
> ~~T The~~ Her Iron necklace and ~~the~~ red sores of ~~my~~ the shoulders
> I do not ~~feel~~ mind,
> The Hopple ~~and ball~~ at ~~my~~ the ancles, ^and tight cuffs at the wrists
> ~~does~~ ^must not detain me
> I ^will go down the river with ^the sight of my bloodshot eyes.
> I {will} go ~~in~~ to the steamboat that paddles^off my ~~wife~~ woman and child
> ~~A~~ I do not stop with my wom[an?] and children,
> I burst ~~down~~ the saloon doors, and crash on
> party of passengers. –
> ~~But for them, I sh too should have been on the steambo~~[at? – page
> cut off]
> ~~I should soon~~

Here Whitman works to turn his poem over to the consciousness and the sensibility of a black slave, allowing himself to be thought by "a negro" and letting his voice emerge from the black slave's mouth. Whitman's attempt is not to speak for the black slave but to speak *as* the black slave. We can read this attempt as a kind of subjugation of the black, who can speak only when the white poet speaks for him, or we can read the attempt as a remarkable recognition of the black's subjectivity, with the poet inhabited by another subjectivity, one that in mid-nineteenth-century America was alien to the white poet. Whether the poem enacts Whitman's domination of the slave or the slave's domination of Whitman – or some endless, tensed identity transfer – it remains one of the most powerful and evocative passages about slavery in American literature.

Two other manuscripts at Virginia allow us to see how painstakingly Whitman revised and re-revised, working toward the amazing passage.

~~Crush~~ Topple down upon him ~~Curse~~ [illegible] Light!₁ for ^you seem to
me ~~I am~~ all one lurid ~~Curse~~ ~~Oath~~ curse
I ~~look down~~ off the river ~~with my bloodshot eyes, after~~
~~I see the steamboat that carries off~~ away ~~my woman. –~~
Damn him! how he does defile me
^This day, or some other, I will have him lie at peace and the like of
him to do my will upon; ~~curse the~~
They shall not ~~hide themselves~~ even ~~in their graves~~ tombs with pennies
on their eyes
I ~~will~~ break the lids off their coffins but what
will ~~would~~ I will have then [?]
I will tear their flesh out from under the
grave-clothes
I will not listen – I will not spare – I ~~will~~
am justified of myself:
~~The I will pursue~~ For a ~~million~~ hundred years ^I will pursue those who
have injured me so much:
Though they ~~cover~~ hide themselves ~~with~~ under the lappets
of God I will ~~drag them there~~ pursue them there.
I will ~~stop~~ drag them out – the ~~the,~~ sweet marches of heaven ^shall be
stopped with
my maledictions. –

Here the passage contains an image of death ("pennies on their eyes")
that Whitman would later transfer to "Song of Myself," so these manuscripts reveal just how interwoven all the poems of the first edition
of *Leaves* were: Whitman again and again moves parts of single manuscripts into multiple poems. In this passage, too, we can see the coffins
and the lappets of the early notebook pages still at work and evolving.

His next draft carries the passage much closer to the version he would
eventually publish, and he even writes "Sleepchasers" in the upper
right-hand corner, indicating that he was already thinking of giving
the poem a distinctive title.

Sleepchasers

~~I am a hell-name and a Curse:~~
~~The~~ Black Lucifer was not dead;
Or if he was, I am his sorrowful, terrible heir:
~~I am Appollyon,~~ I am the God of Revolt – deathless sorrowful vast
scorner of ~~those~~ ^him whoever ~~who rules~~ ^oppresses me,

I will either destroy ~~them~~ him or ~~they~~ he shall release me.

~~Damn him! how he does defile me!~~
~~He~~ Hoppler ^of his own sons; ~~he~~ breeder of children and ~~sells~~ trader them
~~He treats politicians~~ ^Selling his daughters and the breast that ~~he~~ fed his young and ^[illegible] ~~buys a nomination to~~ ^[illegible], ~~great~~ ~~office;~~
~~He~~ Informer against my brother and sister and ~~got~~ took asking pay for their ~~blood,~~ blood, ~~hearts;~~
~~He~~ He Laughed when I looked ^from my iron necklace, after the steam-boat that carried away my woman –

Now the lappets and the coffins are gone, but the "negro" has at this point taken on the identity of "Black Lucifer." By the time of this draft, Whitman has settled on the language for the published version of the passage and has obliterated his own "I" and given the "I" over totally to Black Lucifer. The slave is subject instead of object here, and Lucifer has powerful access to his own subjectivity and agency ("I will either destroy him," he says of his white master, "or he shall release me").

But Lucifer's expression of hate and his vow of action against the slavemaster are not the final words in "The Sleepers." Whitman ends the poem with a vast, unifying catalog, a vision of the universe "duly in order . . . every thing is in its place." This absorptive vision includes, surprisingly, Lucifer now joined with his master, presumably after they have experienced the illumination of their oneness in an emerging democratic sensibility: "The call of the slave is one with the master's call . . . and the master salutes the slave." The image of Lucifer flaring into hatred and violent action is subsumed by the final image that offers a resolution more exalted than violence and hate, a seemingly unlikely resolution of love, understanding, oneness, in which the slaveowner now sees the error of his ways and joins voices with the slave, saluting him in some unspecified gesture of respect. Here at the end of the poem, Whitman comes as close as he ever would to attaining the voice that would speak for the slaves and the masters of slaves – "The diverse shall be no less diverse, but they shall flow and unite . . . they unite now" – but it is a voice that fails to alter the course of American history, as would become painfully clear five years after *Leaves* was published, when the Civil War broke out.

The Lucifer passage lingers in *Leaves* through the first two post-Civil War editions as a kind of vestige of Whitman's antebellum desire to voice the subjectivity of the slave, to give the slave power and agency, and to imagine that that poetic act might be enough to change the slavemaster's perception of slaves, to coerce the slavemasters into recognizing the humanity in those they treated as objects and possessions, as less than human. In the late 1870s, however, as Whitman revised his book for a new edition that would be published in 1881, he made a stunning decision. He deleted the "Lucifer" section of "The Sleepers," crossing it out on his working copy of his 1871–2 edition and marking two "d's" (one in pencil and one emphatically in dark ink) to indicate to the printer to omit the section. (Whitman deleted the George Washington section of the poem at the same time, but then reconsidered and marked "stet" by that section, thus preserving the feminized image of the Father of the Country.) Whitman's decision to remove the Lucifer section meant that one of the great passages about black slaves gaining voice in American poetry vanished from subsequent editions of *Leaves of Grass*. Most reprintings of Whitman's work are made from his final edition, so most copies of "The Sleepers" in print today do not contain one of his most powerful passages.

Whitman's manuscripts and the changes in his various editions offer us a living workshop of his poetic development and his changing ideas about America. The 1855 edition of *Leaves* clearly was a book written for an America that still was wrestling with the issue of slavery, an America that had not yet broken apart in civil war. Slavery is an issue throughout the poems of the first edition, and the opening long poem that became "Song of Myself" is built on a slave escape narrative, from the moment when the speaker houses "the runaway slave" and nurses him ("putting plasters on the galls of his neck and ankles") and feeds him at his own table (*LG 1855*, 19), to the scene where the speaker identifies with the runaway slave who is caught ("I am the hounded slave . . . I wince at the bite of the dogs" [*LG 1855*, 39]). *These* leaves of grass, Whitman says, speak for the ideal of equality, "Growing among black folks as among white" (*LG 1855*, 16). His attempts to fuse with and experience black subjectivity, then, are key components of the book.

Whitman always recalled the first edition of *Leaves of Grass* as appearing, fittingly, on the Fourth of July, as a kind of literary Independence Day: he saw his book as offering a new declaration – a declaration of *inter*dependence – that might hold the United States together. His joy at getting the book published was quickly diminished, however, by the death of his father within a week of the appearance of *Leaves*. Walter Sr had been ill for several years, and though he and Walt had never been particularly close, they had only recently traveled together to West Hills, Long Island, to the old Whitman homestead where Walt was born. Now his father's death along with his older brother Jesse's absence as a merchant marine (and later Jesse's growing violence and mental instability) meant that Walt would become the father-substitute for the family, the person his mother and siblings would turn to for help and guidance. He had already had some experience enacting that role even while Walter Sr was alive; perhaps because of Walter Sr's drinking habits and growing general depression, young Walt had taken on a number of adult responsibilities – buying boots for his brothers, for instance, and holding the title to the family house as early as 1847. Now, however, he became the only person his mother and siblings could turn to.

But even given these growing family burdens, he managed to concentrate on his new book, and, just as he oversaw all the details of its composition and printing, so now did he supervise its distribution and try to control its reception. Even though Whitman claimed that the first edition sold out, the book in fact had very poor sales. He sent copies to a number of well-known writers (including John Greenleaf Whittier, who, legend has it, threw his copy in the fire), but only one responded, and that, fittingly, was Emerson, who recognized in Whitman's work the very spirit and tone and style he had called for in "The Poet." "I greet you at the beginning of a great career," Emerson wrote in his private letter to Whitman, noting that *Leaves of Grass* "meets the demand I am always making of what seemed the sterile and stingy nature, as if too much handiwork, or too much lymph in the temperament, were making our western wits fat and mean." Whitman's was poetry that would literally get the country in shape, Emerson believed, *give* it shape, and help work off its excess of aristocratic fat.

Despite its poor sales, Whitman always loved the first edition of his work like a first child. Over the course of his career, many of his friends expressed – sometimes to his consternation – a preference for the slim first edition over all the larger editions of *Leaves* that would come after. In 1888, he told his friend Horace Traubel, "Do you know, I think almost all the fellows who came first like the first edition above all others. Yet the last edition is as necessary to my scheme as the first edition: no one could be superior to another because all are of equal importance in the fulfillment of the design." But Whitman goes on to say why he does not consider his friends' preference for the 1855 *Leaves* "unreasonable": "there was an immediateness in the 1855 edition, an incisive directness, that was perhaps not repeated in any section of poems afterwards added to the book: a hot, unqualifying temper, an insulting arrogance . . . that would not have been as natural to the periods that followed. We miss that ecstasy of statement in some of the after-work" (*WWC*, 2:225). No one has expressed better than Whitman does here the qualities that so many readers have found in the 1855 *Leaves of Grass*.

Within a few months of producing his first edition of *Leaves*, Whitman was already hard at work on the second edition. He was busy reconceptualizing his book, and he would continue to do so for his whole life. Each edition of *Leaves* is essentially a different book, not just another version of the same book. For his 1856 edition, Whitman added 20 new poems to the original 12. But as the book grew in number of poems, it shrank in page size; the paper for this edition is less than half the size of that of the first. As in the first, no publisher appears in this edition, but the book was in fact printed by Fowler and Wells, the combination phrenology firm, bookseller, and publisher for which Whitman had worked. Fowler and Wells distributed the first edition, and, while they in effect published the second edition, they still did not want their names appearing on the title page of such a controversial work (even though an ad for their various bookselling outlets appears at the back of the volume!).

The second edition demonstrates Whitman's changing attitudes toward his book and the revised goals he now had for his work. He quickly gave up his desire to have spacious pages that would easily accommodate his long and flowing lines, and instead he shrank the book to a "pocket-size" edition. His dream now was to have working people carry his poetry with them and read it during breaks: "to put a book in your pocket and off to the seashore or the forest – that is an ideal pleasure." So he created a book that he hoped would "go into any reasonable pocket," something the first edition clearly would not do. What he ended up with, however, was what he called "the chunky fat book," its cramped pages and tight margins forcing the poet to break his lines frequently so that they fit on the page.

The 1856 edition manifests Emerson's influence on Whitman. As we have noted, Whitman owed a great deal to the great Concord writer and philosopher, whose essay "The Poet" seemed in many ways to prophesy Walt Whitman (some critics would argue that Whitman simply modeled himself on Emerson's essay). Whitman reportedly said that by the mid-1850s he was "simmering, simmering; Emerson brought me to a boil" (quoted in Myerson 1991, 173). If that is true, then this edition is the most furious roiling of the waters. Whitman here prints the supportive letter that Emerson had sent him after reading the 1855 *Leaves* (a letter that Whitman had reprinted in the New York *Tribune*), prints his own 12-page response to Emerson (addressing him as "Master"), and brazenly features Emerson's name and endorsement on the spine of the book – one of the first blurbs in American publishing history. Whitman carefully sketched out plans for the spine, figuring precisely how he wanted to position the carefully selected words from Emerson's letter: "I greet you at the beginning of a great career." This statement appears in gold letters, followed by "R. W. Emerson." Whitman used this emblazoned blurb without Emerson's permission, initiating a controversy that rages to this day, and Emerson, for his part, reluctantly learned to accept such behavior from Whitman (when Emerson loaned his copy of the 1856 edition to a friend, he said that "the inside was worthy [of] attention even though it came from one capable of so misusing the cover"). Of all the important lessons Whitman learned from Emerson, the one that he seems to have most taken to heart was Emerson's definition of "genius" in his essay on "Intellect": "To genius must always go two gifts, the thought and the publication. The first is revelation, always a miracle . . . It affects every thought of man, and goes to fashion every institution. But to make it available, it needs a vehicle or art by which it is conveyed to men" (Emerson 1983, 422). The 1856 edition of *Leaves* is Whitman's carefully orchestrated attempt to convey his radical thought in an Emerson-fueled vehicle.

Beyond the Emerson blurb, the cover of the 1856 edition is a miniature version of the 1855 cover, still green with blind-stamped foliage, but now with an unornamented and inorganic "Leaves of Grass" on the front cover. On the spine, however, the "a" in "Grass" and the "m" in "Whitman" both sprout leaves, and Whitman's sketches for the spine show him playfully pulling roots out of the letters of his title.

In order to generate publicity for the volume, Whitman appended at the back of the book a group of reviews of the first edition – including three he wrote himself, along with a few negative reviews – and called the gathering *Leaves-Droppings*, a pun on "eaves-dropping," the act of listening in on what you're not supposed to be hearing. It's as if he is suggesting that the excerpts are simply overheard comments – good and bad – that others were making about *Leaves*. He was a pioneer of the "any publicity is better than no publicity" strategy. His long public letter to Emerson at the back of the book serves as a kind of apologia for his poetry, much as the preface had in the first edition. Although Whitman would later downplay the influence of Emerson on his work, at this time he had what he later called "Emerson-on-the-brain."

Among the new poems added to this edition was the powerful "Sun-Down Poem," later called "Crossing Brooklyn Ferry." Whitman had provided no titles other than "Leaves of Grass" in 1855, but in 1856 he was doing all he could to make the new edition look and feel different: small pages instead of large, a fat book instead of a thin one, and individualized titles – some of them long and eccentric – for each of his poems. So the untitled introductory poem from the first edition that would eventually be named "Song of Myself" was in 1856 called "Poem of Walt Whitman, an American," and the poem that would become "This Compost" appeared here as "Poem of Wonder at the Resurrection of The Wheat." Some titles seemed to challenge the very bounds of titling by incorporating rolling catalogs like the poems themselves: "To a Foil'd European Revolutionaire" appeared as "Liberty Poem for Asia, Africa, Europe, America, Australia, Cuba, and The Archipelagoes of the Sea." It is as if Whitman was setting out to counter some of the early criticism that he was not really writing poetry at all: the review in *Life Illustrated*, for example, called Whitman's work "lines of rhythmical prose, or a series of *utterances* (we know not what else to call them)," and even Emerson in his positive letter to Whitman avoided the use of the term "poetry," calling Whitman's work instead "wit and wisdom." So Whitman put the word "Poem" in the title of all 32 works in the 1856 *Leaves*. Like them or not, he seemed to be saying, they *are* poems, and more and more of them were on the way. But, despite his efforts to remake his book, the results were depressingly the same: sales of the thousand copies that were printed were even poorer than for the first edition.

CHAPTER 4

Intimate Script and the New American Bible: "Calamus" and the Making of the 1860 *Leaves of Grass*

From 1855 through 1860, Whitman was working hard at becoming a poet by forging literary connections: he entered the literary world in a way he never had as a fiction writer or journalist, meeting some of the nation's best-known writers, beginning to socialize with a literary and artistic crowd, and cultivating an image as an artist. He was gradually shifting his professional identity from newspaperman to creative and controversial poet. Emerson had come to visit him at the end of 1855 (they went back to Emerson's room at the elegant Astor Hotel, where Whitman – dressed as informally as he was in his frontispiece portrait – was denied admission). This was the first of many meetings the two would have over the next twenty-five years, as their relationship settled into one of grudging respect for each other mixed with mutual suspicion. The next year, Henry David Thoreau and Bronson Alcott visited Whitman's home (Alcott described Thoreau and Whitman as each "surveying the other curiously, like two beasts, each wondering what the other would do"). Whitman also came to befriend a number of visual artists, like the sculptor Henry Kirke Brown, the painter Elihu Vedder, and the photographer Gabriel Harrison. And he came to know a number of women's rights activists and writers, some of whom became ardent readers and supporters of *Leaves of Grass*. As Sherry Ceniza (1998) has demonstrated, he became particularly close to Abby Price, Paulina Wright Davis, Sarah Tyndale, and Sara Payson Willis (who, under the pseudonym Fanny Fern, wrote a popular newspaper column and many popular books, including *Fern Leaves from Fanny's Portfolio* [1853], the cover of which Whitman imitated for his first edition of *Leaves*). These women's radical ideas about sexual equality had a growing impact on Whitman's poetry. He knew a number of abolitionist writers at this time, including Moncure Conway, and Whitman wrote some vitriolic attacks on the fugitive slave law and the moral bankruptcy of American politics, but these pieces (notably "The Eighteenth Presidency!") were never published and remain vestiges of yet another career – stump speaker, political pundit – that he flirted with but never pursued.

Whitman also began in the late 1850s to become a regular at Pfaff's saloon, a favorite hangout for bohemian artists in New York. He had worked for a couple of years for the Brooklyn *Daily Times*, a Free-Soil newspaper that opposed the expansion of slavery into the Western territories, until the middle of 1859, when, once again, a disagreement with the newspaper's owner led to his dismissal. At Pfaff's, Whitman the former temperance writer began a couple of years of unemployed carousing; he was clearly remaking his image, going to bars more often than he had since he left New Orleans a decade earlier. At Pfaff's, he mingled with figures like Henry Clapp, the influential editor of the anti-establishment *Saturday Press*, who would help publicize Whitman's work in many ways, including publishing in 1859 an early version of "Out of the Cradle Endlessly Rocking." Whitman also became friends at Pfaff's with many writers, some well known at the time: Ada Clare, Fitz-James O'Brien, George Arnold, and Edmund Clarence Stedman. It was here, too, that a young William Dean Howells met Whitman; Howells recalled this meeting many years later, when he made it clear that Whitman had already by the time of their meeting become something of a celebrity, even if his fame was largely the infamy resulting from what many considered to be his obscene writings ("foul work" filled with "libidinousness," scolded the *Christian Examiner*). Whitman and Ada Clare, known as the "queen of Bohemia" (she had an illegitimate child and proudly proclaimed herself an unmarried mother), became two of the most notorious figures at the beer hall, flouting convention and decorum.

It was at Pfaff's, too, that Whitman joined the "Fred Gray Association," a loose confederation of young men who seemed anxious to explore new possibilities of male–male affection. It may have been there that he met Fred Vaughan, an intriguing mystery-figure in Whitman biography. Whitman and Vaughan, a young Irish stage driver, clearly had an intense relationship at this time, perhaps inspiring the sequence of homoerotic love poems Whitman called "Live Oak, with Moss," poems that would become the heart of his "Calamus" cluster, which would appear in the 1860 edition of *Leaves*. These poems record a despair about the failure of the relationship, and the loss of Whitman's bond with Vaughan – who soon married, had four children, and would only sporadically keep in touch with Whitman – was clearly the source of some deep unhappiness for the poet:

> Hours continuing long, sore and heavy-hearted,
> Hours of the dusk, when I withdraw to a lonesome and unfrequented spot, seating myself, leaning my face in my hands,
> Hours sleepless, deep in the night, when I go forth, speeding swiftly the country roads, or through the city streets, or pacing miles and miles, stifling plaintive cries,
> Hours discouraged, distracted, – For he, the one I cannot content myself without – soon I saw him content himself without me,
> Hours when I am forgotten – . . .
> Sullen and suffering hours – (I am ashamed – but it is useless – I am what I am;). (Bowers 1955, 82)

"Live Oak, with Moss" was composed as a sequence of 12 sonnet-like love poems. Whitman took care with this powerful sequence, inscribing fair-copy versions of the poems into a notebook. (These manuscripts are far less messy than his typical poetry drafts.) He never published the sequence as such. Instead, he tore the individual leaves out of the notebook, revised some of the poems, and altered their order when he published the much longer 45-poem "Calamus" cluster. These changes made a once fairly clear narrative of love and loss far less clear. Whitman may have concluded that the poems, frank in their treatment of male–male love, were too risky, revealing, or compromising. Most critics have concluded that the "Calamus" poems are an attempt to disguise what seems like a much more frank and direct portrayal of a male–male love relationship in the "Live

Oak" sequence. Whatever is the case, these poems bring us to one of the most controversial and most discussed aspects of Whitman's work in the past several decades – the nature of his sexuality, and the meaning of his poems that celebrate affection between males. We need to look for a moment at some of the lively critical debate that has raged in recent years about this issue.

Despite the daring and originality of Whitman's achievement in the "Live Oak" poems, critics have been slow to appreciate it. He himself didn't help much: he said next to nothing about the sequence in later years, and if a love affair does lie behind the sequence, he commented on it only obliquely. In fact, the existence of the "Live Oak" sequence was utterly unknown to scholars until 1953, when Fredson Bowers discovered it while working with manuscripts now at the University of Virginia. For various reasons, including the reluctance of scholars at that time to discuss same-sex love, Bowers's discovery was left largely ignored and its implications unexplored.

We cannot know with certainty about Whitman's romantic life in the late 1850s. As Carroll Smith-Rosenberg (1986) and other cultural historians have noted, it is a tricky matter to draw inferences from nineteenth-century discourses of intimacy. The coded expressions and indirections of love talk are not easy to decipher, and expressions of fervent attachment may or may not imply the same level of sexual intimacy as such an expression would imply in our own time. It is good to remember that we inescapably read Whitman from a post-Freudian, post-Stonewall perspective, a perspective that is simultaneously distorting and illuminating. It has only been recently that sexual historians like Jonathan Ned Katz have offered detailed examinations of sexual behavior in the nineteenth century. Katz, in his study *Love Stories*, effectively creates a historical panorama of nineteenth-century male–male sexual behavior and demonstrates how American culture at the time worked to keep "romantic, spiritual love" between men totally separate from sexual lust between men. Whitman becomes for Katz the breakthrough figure who "began to explore the erotic intimacy of men and to invent a new language to express it" (Katz 2001, 122). Until Whitman, Katz argues, men could express love toward other men, or they could have sex with other men, but they could not express doing both together. Whitman discovered a way to talk about men loving men sexually. It may be that, before the twentieth century, there were homosexual acts but no homosexuals, but Katz shows there *were* "sodomites" – it's just that that particular identity did not allow for love relationships: a sodomite was constructed as a monster, a freak of nature. Whitman in this sense, then, *did* invent gay identity, because, after him, it became possible to express love through acts that before had been cast outside of love's reach. He had a number of such affectionate bondings – his 1850s relationship with Fred Vaughan; his numerous affectional relationships with young Civil War soldiers; his well-known partnership with Peter Doyle (see chapter 5); his troubled and intense relationship with Harry Stafford (see chapter 6); and less well-documented relationships with Edward Cattell, Bill Duckett, and Warren Fritzinger (see chapters 6 and 7).

It is striking that Whitman turned his attention to working out a language of male–male affection at precisely the historical moment that male–male violence was about to break out across the country, as the US moved inexorably toward civil war. What may seem at first an avoidance of the country's divisive politics and a turn instead to personal concerns can in fact be viewed as Whitman's powerful attempt to affirm the necessity of males caring for other males as a basis for a successful democracy, as a foundation for a republic that perhaps too often inculcates in its youth the idea of fierce competition as its central value.

In this light, the "Live Oak" poems are revelatory. Still, to find satisfactory language with which to discuss Whitman's love poetry is difficult: one would like to avoid both the squeamishness of euphemisms and the inaccuracy of anachronism. The critic Alan Helms, for example, talks about Whitman as a man who had "come out as America's first self-identified 'homosexual'" (Martin 1992, 186). Helms then suggests that we ought to "at last begin where Whitman himself began" (Martin 1992, 186), implying that he will be sensitive to Whitman's historical context. Although Helms puts the term *homosexual* in quotation marks, suggesting that he uses the word advisedly, he doesn't explicitly talk about the paradox (not to say anachronistic impossibility) of Whitman becoming a "self-identified 'homosexual'" a decade before the word *homosexual* was coined by the German-Hungarian journalist Karl Maria Kertbeny, in a letter written to the sexologist Karl Heinrich Ulrichs. (The earliest known usage of *homosexual* in a US text was in the Chicago *Medical Recorder*, May 1892.) Nor does Helms comment on the problems of thinking of "coming out" as a transhistorical phenomenon and not as something that is very much culturally and temporally conditioned. In many ways Whitman's culture was *not* like that of the modern-day US. His culture was far more accepting of open displays of same-sex affection. Moreover, male–male love, though not encouraged, had not been pathologized as it would be later in the nineteenth century.

In similar fashion one has to question Hershel Parker's description of the "Live Oak" sequence as a "gay manifesto" (Parker 1996, 145), not only because the meaning of the sequence was as much obscured as trumpeted by Whitman, but also because "gay" is a term as anachronistic as "homosexual" to describe Whitman in the 1850s. The poet himself developed a rich terminology to describe love between men, and we do well to follow his lead in opting for terms such as "manly love," "adhesiveness," and the like. His key term in this regard was "calamus," referring to an aromatic marsh-plant sometimes known as sweet-flag; the phallic shape of the cylindrical, spike flower of calamus made it richly suggestive. Whitman's choice of terms do not prohibit one from concluding that he engaged in genital sexuality with his male lover, but neither do they require that conclusion. The terms themselves retain an insistent mystery, a feature Whitman prized highly in his love poetry.

As Steven Olsen-Smith and Hershel Parker point out, the tendency in Whitman criticism has been to speak inexactly about clusters and even individual poems (Olsen-Smith and Parker 1997). Critics frequently refer to, say, "Out of the Cradle Endlessly Rocking" or "Calamus" without specifying which edition is meant and sometimes with the implication that the remark holds for all versions of a poem or cluster. Given Whitman's current status as icon of gay America, and given the imprecision with which critics have typically referred to Whitman texts, an explosive mix has been brewing in Whitman criticism.

In 1992, Alan Helms published the "Live Oak with Moss" sequence in a book of essays on Whitman (Martin 1992). But Helms's choice of texts created a small critical storm. He articulated his editorial policy as follows: "I give the 'Live Oak' poems in their first published form – that is, as they appeared in the third *Leaves of Grass* in 1860 in the form Whitman approved for publication. I've simply removed them from 'Calamus' and restored them to Whitman's original order" (Martin 1992, 187). Helms's editing of the sequence received blistering criticism in 1996 from Hershel Parker, who pointed out that Helms had put forward a combined text different than Whitman had ever compiled (the revised 1860 versions of the "Live Oak" poems in the original sequence's order). Parker notes that "there is nothing merely 'academic' about the distinction between a correct text and an incorrect text of this Whitman sequence" (Parker 1996, 159). He insists that Helms has misinterpreted Whitman by reading a spurious text and that he himself rather than Helms offers the "genuine" or the "real" "Live Oak, with Moss" by publishing a transcription of the manuscripts in the *Norton Anthology of American Literature* (Baym 1994).

As it happens, we think Parker gets the better of the textual editing argument, though his language is unnecessarily harsh. He offers a careful transcription of Whitman's text, a closer approximation to what the poet originally inscribed in "Live Oak," though Parker, curiously, invokes a language of authenticity that is typically reserved only for original artifacts (such as the actual manuscripts themselves, now housed in the University of Virginia Special Collections). One can see why the stakes are high: as Helms points out, it is possible to argue that "Live Oak" as opposed to the fuzzier "Calamus" is the "only sustained treatment of homosexual love in all of his poetry" (p. 186). How those documents are edited, taught, and interpreted is a matter, then, of considerable academic and social importance. Helms, reading his particular textual version of "Live Oak," found the poems to trace a "sad journey" and offer a "narrative of homophobic oppression" (pp. 191, 190). Parker, reading *his* textual version of the sequence, found almost the opposite – an affirming "gay manifesto" contained in an "ebullient narrative" (p. 155) in which the speaker overcomes the abandonment by his lover and, secure in his identity, moves on.

This critical debate underscores the importance of Whitman's often overlooked poetry manuscripts. Lying behind all of the familiar printed poems in *Leaves of Grass* are manuscripts that tell originating stories of how and why he ended up publishing what he did. A comparison of the "Live Oak" sequence with the various published "Calamus" sequences (starting in the 1860 *Leaves* and developing through the 1881 edition) reveals how he turned a sequence of poems mainly about a personal affair into a longer sequence that maintains his concern with male–male affection, while also widening that concern to the national crisis of Union that the US faced at this time.

Whitman knew that these feelings he experienced – feelings that at the time literally had no name – were important, not just for himself but for the developing nation. They might be thought of as his "calamus emotions," manifested in a protean set of relationships that extended throughout his life from at least the late 1850s on. It is sometimes forgotten that he kept returning to and redefining the term "calamus" after its initial appearance in print in the 1860 edition of *Leaves*. In the 1860 "Calamus," the cluster opens by announcing Whitman's new decision to "proceed, for all who are, or have been, young men, / To tell the secret of my nights and days, / To celebrate the need of comrades" (*LG 1860*, 342), and he goes on to try to imagine what a country would be like that embodied "[t]he institution of the dear love of comrades" (*LG 1860*, 368). Betsy Erkkila has argued convincingly that we can best understand the "Calamus" poems not as expressions of Whitman's private life as distinct from his more "public" poems, but rather as the first expression of "a homosexual republic," a new conception of American democracy that joins non-procreative sexual feelings with the sense of comradeship and democratic union (Erkkila 1994).

So, by 1876, Whitman would define the "Calamus" poems as very much political poems:

> [I]mportant as they are in my purpose as emotional expressions for humanity, the special meaning of the *Calamus* cluster of Leaves of Grass . . . mainly resides in its Political significance. In my opinion it is by a fervent, accepted development of Comradeship, the beautiful and sane affection of man for man, latent in all the young fellows, North and South, East and West – it is by this, I say, and by what goes directly and indirectly along with it, that the United States of the future, (I cannot too often repeat,) are to be most effectually welded together, intercalated, anneal'd into a Living Union. (*LG*, 753)

Whitman would continue to come back to and rethink the implications of the term throughout his life. Even as late as 1890, when confronted with the charge that "the subject of 'Calamus'" might be understood as condoning homosexual behavior, "verging upon the licentiousness of the Greek," his response was to once again reconstruct the meaning of the term:

> Yes I see! And indeed I can see how it might be opened to such an interpretation. But I can say further, that in the ten thousand who for many years now have stood ready to make any possible charge against me – to seize any pretext or suspicion – none have raised this objection;

perhaps all the more reason for having it urged now. "Calamus" is a Latin word – much used in Old English writing, however. I like it much – it is to me, for my intentions, indispensible – the sun revolves about it, it is a timber of the ship – not there alone in that one series of poems, but in all, belonging to all. It is one of the United States – it is the quality which makes the states whole – it is the thin thread – but, oh! the significant thread! – by which the nation is held together, a chain of comrades; it could no more be dispensed with than the ship entire. I know no country anyhow in which comradeship is so far developed as here – here, among the mechanic classes. (*WWC*, 6:342–3)

Without denying the homosexual interpretation of "Calamus," then, Whitman deftly dilates its meaning into a wide social realm and insists that it is essential to his entire poetic project. His suggestion that "Calamus" is "indispensible . . . a timber of the ship" recalls his line in "Song of Myself" – "a kelson of the creation is love" (*LG*, 33) – and reminds us how much he sees love, in whatever forms it takes, as the foundational structural beam of America's ship of state.

Near the end of the "Calamus" cluster is the short poem called "I Dream'd in a Dream":

> I dream'd in a dream I saw a city invincible to the attacks of the whole
>   of the rest of the earth,
> I dream'd that was the new city of Friends,
> Nothing was greater there than the quality of robust love, it led the
>   rest,
> It was seen every hour in the actions of the men of that city,
> And in all their looks and words. (*LG*, 133)

Here is a dream of the "homosexual republic." And yet it is a dream that transcends sexual behavior and choice and imagines a city founded on "robust love," suggesting not just love between men and women, but between men and men and women and women. Lines from this poem are in fact carved into the City Hall of Camden, New Jersey, where Whitman lived during the last years of his life, as an indication of a civic ideal.

The 1860 edition of *Leaves*, by including the "Calamus" poems and the related "Enfans d'Adam" cluster (later titled "Children of Adam"), alters the purposes and goals of Whitman's poetic project. These poems introduced the issue of sexuality into the book in even more direct and frank ways than the 1855 and 1856 editions had. Many critics have claimed that the "Enfans d'Adam" poems celebrate heterosexual passion while the "Calamus" poems focus on homosexual desire. But in fact the division is not that clear, and the manuscripts indicate that the poems in both clusters were written at about the same time and were intermingled in Whitman's mind. Many of the "Calamus" poems are gender-neutral, and their expression of desire can work effectively for any affectional relationship, with the language unspecific enough to fit any reader's needs: "Passing stranger! you do not know how longingly I look upon you, / You must be he I was seeking, or she I was seeking, (it comes to me as of a dream,) / I have somewhere surely lived a life of joy with you" (*LG*, 127).

It is the desire of love, of one person to care deeply for another, that Whitman is concerned about, at precisely the time in the nation's history when brothers were about to begin to kill brothers, and fathers sons, and cousins cousins. He had been concerned for many years about the paucity of words in the English language for love relationships, words that signaled more than simple friendship. He wrote in some mid-1850s notes he made on language: "This is to be said among the young men of These States, that with a wonderful tenacity of friendship, and passionate fondness for their friends, and always a manly readiness to make friends, they yet have remarkably few words of names for the friendly sentiments ... they never give words to their most ardent friendships" (*AP*, 15). Intensification of affectional bonds became a foundation for Whitman's poetry and for his vision of a perfected democracy, and so sexual expressions of affection had to be broken loose from American Puritanical notions that sex was only for procreation: sexual desire, Whitman realized, was a powerful force for love across all kinds of boundaries and had to be more openly expressed in America's literature than it had been before.

Whitman's remade self-image is evident on the frontispiece of the new edition of *Leaves* that appeared in 1860. It would be the only time he used this portrait, an engraving based on a painting done by his artist friend Charles Hine. Whitman's friends called it the "Byronic portrait," and Whitman does look more like the conventional image of a poet – with coiffure and cravat – than he ever did before or after. This is the portrait of an artist who has devoted significant time to his image and one who has also clearly enjoyed his growing notoriety among the arty crowd at Pfaff's.

Ever since the 1856 edition appeared, Whitman had been writing poems at a furious pace; within a year of the 1856 edition's appearance, he wrote nearly seventy new poems. He continued to have them set in type by the Rome brothers and other printer friends, as if he assumed that he would inevitably be publishing them himself, since no commercial publisher had indicated an interest in his book. But there was another reason he set his poems in type: at a certain point in his revision process, he preferred to deal with his poems in printed form instead of in manuscript. He often would continue to revise directly on printed versions of his poetry; for him, poetry was very much a *public* act, and until the poem was in print he did not consider it fully realized as a poem. Although he did painstaking work on his poems in manuscript, the poetic manuscripts themselves were never sacred objects for Whitman, who often simply discarded them; getting the poem set in type was the most important step in allowing it to begin to do its cultural work.

In 1860, while the nation seemed to be moving inexorably toward a major crisis between the slaveholding and free states, Whitman's poetic fortunes took a positive turn. In February, he received a letter from the Boston publishers William Thayer and Charles Eldridge, whose aggressive new publishing house specialized in abolitionist literature; they wanted to become the publishers of the new edition of *Leaves of Grass*. Whitman, feeling confirmed as an authentic poet now that he had been offered actual royalties, readily agreed, and Thayer and Eldridge invested heavily in the stereotype plates for Whitman's idiosyncratic book – over 450 pages of varied typeface and odd decorative motifs, a visually chaotic volume all carefully tended to by Whitman, who traveled to Boston to oversee the printing. It was an exciting and foreboding time. Thayer and Eldridge – both strong antislavery militants – made their initial publishing impact by issuing James Redpath's incendiary *Public Life of Capt. John Brown* just weeks after Brown had been executed for his attack on the US Arsenal at Harper's Ferry, and had immediately become for many Northerners the great martyr to the antislavery cause. Within days of signing up Whitman, Thayer and Eldridge also issued a contract to William Douglas O'Connor to write an antislavery novel, and so it was through this connection with his Boston publishers that Whitman was first to meet O'Connor, who would become his ardent defender and lifelong friend.

This was Whitman's first trip to Boston, then considered the literary capital of the nation. Whitman is a major part of the reason that America's literary center moved from Boston to New York in the second half of the nineteenth century, but in 1860 the superior power of Boston was still evident in its influential publishing houses, its important journals (including the new *Atlantic Monthly*), and its venerable authors (including Henry Wadsworth Longfellow, whom Whitman met briefly while in town). Whitman was proud of the "immense sensation" he caused in the generally formal streets of Boston: "Every body here is so like everybody else – and I am Walt Whitman!" (*Corr.*, 1:49–50).

And, of course, Boston was the city of Emerson, who came to see Whitman shortly after his arrival in the city in March. In one of the most celebrated meetings of major American writers, the Boston Brahmin and the Yankee rowdy strolled together on the Boston Common, while Emerson tried to convince Whitman to remove from his Boston edition the new "Enfans d'Adam" cluster of poems, works that portrayed the human body more explicitly and in more direct sexual terms than any previous American poems. Whitman remained firm in the belief, as he later recalled, "that the sexual passion in itself, while normal and unperverted, is inherently legitimate, creditable, not necessarily an improper theme for poet." "*That*," he insisted, "is what I felt in my inmost brain and heart, when I only answer'd Emerson's vehement arguments with silence, under the old elms of Boston Common" (*PW*, 2:493–4). Emerson's caution notwithstanding, the body – the *entire* body – would be Whitman's theme, and he would not shy away from any part of it, not discriminate or marginalize or form hierarchies of bodily parts any more than he would of the diverse people making up the American nation. His democratic belief in the importance of all the parts of any whole was central to his vision: the genitals and the armpits were as essential to the fullness of identity as the brain and the soul, just as, in a democracy, the poorest and most despised citizens were as important as the rich and famous. This, at any rate, was the theory of radical union and equality that generated Whitman's work.

So he ignored Emerson's advice and published the "Enfans d'Adam" poems in the 1860 edition along with his "Calamus" cluster. The body remained very much Whitman's subject, but it was never separate from the body of the text, and he always set out not just to write about sensual embrace but also to *enact* the physical embrace of poet and reader. Whitman became a master of sexual politics, but his sexual politics was always intertwined with his textual politics. *Leaves of Grass* was not a book that set out to shock the reader so much as to *merge* with the reader and make him or her more aware of the body each reader inhabited, to convince us that the body and soul were conjoined and inseparable, just as Whitman's ideas were embodied in words that had physical body in the ink and paper that readers held physically in their hands. Ideas, Whitman's poems insist, pass from one person to another not in some ethereal process, but through the bodies of texts, through the muscular operations of tongues and hands and eyes, through the material objects of books.

So, when Whitman writes in the "Enfans d'Adam" poem later entitled "A Woman Waits for Me":

> Through you I drain the pent-up rivers of myself,
> In you I wrap a thousand onward years,
> On you I graft the grafts of the best-beloved of me and of America,
> The drops I distil upon you shall grow fierce and athletic girls, new artists, musicians, and singers,
> The babes I beget upon you are to beget babes in their turn,
> I shall demand perfect men and women out of my love-spendings,
> I shall expect them to interpenetrate with others, as I and you interpenetrate now, (*LG 1860*, 304)

he is at once evoking an explicit sexual experience *and* the intimate reading experience that the reader is experiencing at this moment. The lover is pictured "interpenetrating" with the speaker of the poem, just as the reader – at the moment of reading – "interpenetrates now" with the speaker's words. Reading is itself an intimate experience, a kind of sexual act of interpenetration. In sexual intercourse, the sperm is the seed planted in the womb to create babies, while in reading, the words of the poem are the seeds planted in the reader's mind to create new ideas. The result of both acts will be new gestations, "fierce and athletic girls, new artists, musicians, and singers": Whitman imagines his radical poems having the effect of creating new individuals, of generating new artists and poets. Even though the poem fantasizes from a male perspective about taking a woman sexually by force ("I make my way, / I am stern, acrid, large, undissuadable . . . / I do not hurt you any more than is necessary for you" [*LG 1860*, 303]), it was nonetheless a favorite of some nineteenth-century women reformers, both for the way it celebrated female sexuality ("Without shame the man I like knows and avows the deliciousness of his sex, / Without shame the woman I like knows and avows hers" [*LG 1860*, 302]) and for the way it projected a new kind of independent American woman ("They know how to swim, row, ride, wrestle, shoot, run, strike, retreat, advance, resist, defend themselves, / They are ultimate in their own right – they are calm, clear, well-possessed of themselves" [*LG 1860*, 303]).

Today, as we've indicated, Whitman's "Calamus" poems still stir up controversy. In the nineteenth century, however, they did not cause as much sensation as "Enfans d'Adam" (or "Children of Adam") because, even though they portrayed same-sex affection, they were only mildly sensual, evoking handholding, hugging, and kissing, while the "Children of Adam" poems evoked a more explicit genital sexuality. Emerson and others were apparently unfazed by "Calamus" and focused their disapprobation on "Children of Adam." Only later in the century, when homosexuality began to be formulated in medical and psychological circles as an aberrant personality type, did the "Calamus" poems begin to be read by some as dangerous and "abnormal" and by others as brave early expressions of gay identity.

These were the two most prominent clusters of the 1860 edition of *Leaves*, but throughout this edition Whitman focused on rearranging his poems in various clusters and groupings. As we have seen, as early as 1855 he began experimenting with clusters, but now he definitely settled on cluster arrangements as the most effective way to organize his work, though his notion of particular clusters changed from edition to edition as he added, deleted, and rearranged his poems in patterns that often alter their meanings and recontextualize their significance. In addition to "Calamus" and "Enfans d'Adam," the 1860 edition contained clusters called "Chants Democratic and Native American" and "Messenger Leaves," and another named the same as the book, "Leaves of Grass." This edition also contained the first book printings of "Starting from Paumanok" (here called "Proto-Leaf") and "Out of the Cradle Endlessly Rocking" (here called "A Word Out of the Sea"), along with over 120 other new poems. He also revised many of his other poems, including "Song of Myself" (here called simply "Walt Whitman"), and throughout the book he numbered his poetic verses, creating a biblical effect.

The Thayer and Eldridge edition is a big book – 456 pages – and it has the feel of a monumental work, something Whitman was by this point in his career trying consciously to produce. He had been writing in his notes about his desire to create "the New Bible," a Bible for American democracy that would reconfigure morality on radically democratic terms. In his own working copy of the 1860 edition of *Leaves*, Whitman carefully noted the number of words in the Bible (895,752), the number of words in the New Testament (212,000), and the number of words in the "Boston ed. Leaves of Grass" (150,500). He had achieved by his own count an impressive amount of verbiage but was still quite a ways from overtaking his ancient rival.

This edition is the first not to have a green binding. Whitman bound the 1860 book in several different colors – from yellowish brown to reddish orange. On the front cover "Leaves of Grass" appears blind-stamped around a blind-stamped globe, revealing the Western hemisphere, floating in clouds. The letters of "Leaves of Grass" have stylized roots or vines emerging from the "L" and "G." On the spine, "Leaves of Grass" is gold-stamped, and at the bottom of the spine is the name "Walt Whitman," blind-stamped as if to suggest that the poet still had some reticence about trumpeting his individual identity; it is the first time his name appeared on a cover. Above the name is a blind-stamped hand with a butterfly perched on a pointing finger; this emblem of the union of man and nature, of the body and the soul, reappears several times in the book, and some years later Whitman brought the figure to life by posing for a photograph with a fake butterfly perched on his finger. The 1860 edition sold fairly well, with the first printing of 1,000 copies quickly exhausted and an additional printing (totaling at least 1,000 and perhaps as many as 3,000 or 4,000 more copies) promptly ordered by Thayer and Eldridge. The 1860 edition received many reviews, most of them positive, particularly those by women readers, who, it seems, were more exhilarated than offended by Whitman's candid images of sex and the body, and who welcomed his language of equality between the sexes, his attempts to sing "The Female equally with the Male."

Whitman's time in Boston – the first extended period he had been away from New York since his trip to New Orleans 12 years earlier – was a transforming experience. He was surprised by the way African Americans were treated much more fairly and more as equals than was the case in New York, sharing tables with whites at eating houses, working next to whites in printing offices, and serving on juries. He also met a number of abolitionist writers who would soon become close friends and supporters, including O'Connor and John Townsend Trowbridge, both of whom would later write at length about Whitman. When he returned to New York at the end of May, his mood was ebullient. He was now a recognized author; the Boston papers had run feature stories about his visit to the city, and photographers had asked to photograph him (not only did he have a growing notoriety, he was a striking physical specimen at over six feet in height – especially tall for the time – with long, already graying hair and beard). All summer long he read reviews of his work in prominent newspapers and journals. And in November, his young publishers announced that his new project, a book of poems he called *Banner at Day-Break*, would be forthcoming. The projected title indicated that Whitman was turning his attention to war.

CHAPTER 5

Blood-Stained Memoranda

Whitman's fortunes turned unexpectedly good early in 1860 only to turn unexpectedly bad. The deteriorating national situation made any business investment risky, and his publisher for the 1860 edition, Thayer and Eldridge, compounded the problem by making a number of bad business decisions. At the beginning of 1861, they declared bankruptcy and sold the plates of *Leaves* to Boston publisher Richard Worthington, who would continue to publish pirated copies of this edition for decades, creating difficulties for Whitman every time he tried to market a new edition. Because of the large number of copies that Thayer and Eldridge initially printed, combined with Worthington's ongoing piracy, the 1860 edition became the most commonly available version of *Leaves* for the next twenty years and diluted the impact (as well as depressing the sales) of Whitman's subsequent editions.

Whitman had dated the title page of his 1860 *Leaves* "1860–61," as if he anticipated the liminal nature of that moment in American history – the fragile moment, between a year of peace and a year of war. In February 1861 he saw Abraham Lincoln pass through New York on the way to his inauguration, and in April Whitman was walking home from an opera performance when he bought a newspaper and read the headlines about Southern forces firing on Fort Sumter. He witnessed a group gathering in the New York streets that night as those with newspapers read the story aloud to the others in the crowd. Even though no one anticipated the full extent of what was to come – Whitman, like many others, thought the struggle would be over in sixty days or so – the nation was in fact slipping into four years of the bloodiest fighting it would ever know. A few days after the firing on Fort Sumter, Whitman recorded in his journal his resolution "to inaugurate for myself a pure, perfect, sweet, cleanblooded, robust body by ignoring all drinks but water and pure milk – and all fat meats, late suppers – a great body – a purged, cleansed, spiritualized, invigorated body" (quoted in Kaplan 1980, 262). It was as if he wished to banish any sense of complacency, to cease his Pfaff's beerhall habits and bohemian ways, and to prepare himself for the challenges that now faced the divided nation. But it would take Whitman some time before he was able to discern the form his war sacrifice would take.

Whitman's brother George immediately enlisted in the Union Army and would serve for the duration of the war, fighting in many of the major battles; he eventually was incarcerated as a prisoner of war in Danville, Virginia. George had a distinguished career as a soldier and left the service as a lieutenant colonel; his descriptions of his war experiences provided Walt with many of his insights into the nature of the war and of soldiers' feelings. Whitman's chronically ill brother Andrew would also enlist but would serve only three months in 1862 before dying, probably of tuberculosis, in 1863. Walt's other brothers – the hot-tempered Jesse (whom Whitman had to have committed to an insane asylum in 1864 after he physically attacked his mother), the recently married Jeff (on whom fell the burden of caring for the extended family, including his own infant daughter), and the mentally enfeebled Eddy – did not enlist, and neither did Walt, who was already in his early forties when the war began (very few men beyond their twenties volunteered for service in the war).

One of the haziest periods of Whitman's life, in fact, is the first year and a half of the war. He stayed in New York and Brooklyn, writing some extended newspaper pieces about the history of Brooklyn for the Brooklyn *Daily Standard*; these pieces, called "Brooklyniana" and consisting of 25 lengthy installments, form a book-length anecdotal history of the city Whitman knew so well but was now about to leave – he would return only occasionally for brief visits. It was during this period that he first encountered casualties of the war that was already lasting far longer than anyone had anticipated. He began visiting wounded soldiers who were moved to New York hospitals, and he wrote about them in a series called "City Photographs" that he published in the New York *Leader* in 1862.

Whitman had in fact been visiting Broadway Hospital for several years, comforting injured stage drivers and ferryboat workers (serious injuries in the chaotic transportation industry in New York at the time were common). While he was enamored of the idea of having literary figures as friends, Whitman's true preference for companions had always been and would continue to be working-class men, especially those who worked on the omnibuses and the ferries ("all my ferry friends," as he called them), where he enjoyed the endless rhythms of movement, the open road, the back-and-forth journeys, with good companions. He reveled in the energy and pleasure of travel instead of worrying about destinations: "I cross'd and recross'd, merely for pleasure," he wrote of his trips on the ferry (*PW*, 1:186). He remembered fondly the "immense qualities, largely animal" of the colorful omnibus drivers, whose company he said he enjoyed "for comradeship, and sometimes affection" as he would ride "the whole length of Broadway," listening to the stories of the driver and conductor, or "declaiming some stormy passage" from one of his favorite Shakespeare plays (*PW*, 1:18–19).

So his hospital visits began with a kind of obligation of friendship to the injured transportation workers, and, as the Civil War began taking its toll, wounded soldiers joined the transportation workers on Whitman's frequent rounds. These soldiers came from all over the country, and their reminiscences of home taught Whitman about the breadth and diversity of the growing nation. He developed an idiosyncratic style of informal personal nursing, writing down stories the patients told him, giving them small gifts, writing letters for them, holding them, comforting them, and kissing them. His purpose, he wrote, was "just to help cheer and change a little the monotony of their sickness and confinement," though he found that their effect on him was every bit as rewarding as his on them, for the wounded and maimed young men aroused in him "friendly interest and sympathy," and he said some of "the most agreeable evenings of my life" were spent in hospitals (Glicksberg 1963, 42). By 1861, his New York hospital visits had prepared him for the draining ordeal he was about to face when he went to Washington, DC, where he would nurse thousands of injured soldiers in the makeshift hospitals there. Whitman once said that, had he not become a writer, he would have become a doctor, and at Broadway Hospital he developed close friendships with many of the physicians, even occasionally assisting them in surgery.

His fascination with the body, so evident in his poetry, was intricately bound to his attraction to medicine and to the hospitals, where he learned to face bodily disfigurations and gained the ability to see beyond wounds and illness to the human personalities that persisted through the pain and humiliation. It was a skill he would need in abundance over the next three years as he began yet another career.

With the nation now locked in an extended war, all of Whitman's deepest concerns and beliefs were under attack. *Leaves of Grass* had been built on a faith in union, wholeness, the ability of a self and a nation to contain contradictions and absorb diversity; now the United States had come apart, and Whitman's very project was in danger of becoming an anachronism as the Southern states sought to divide the country in two. *Leaves* had been built, too, on a belief in the power of affection to overcome division and competition; his "Calamus" vision, as we have seen, was of a "continent indissoluble" with "inseparable cities" all joined by "the life-long love of comrades" (*LG*, 117). But now the young men of America were killing each other in bloody battles; fathers were killing sons, sons fathers, brothers brothers. Whitman's prospects for his "new Bible" that would bind a nation, build an affectionate democracy, and guide a citizenry to celebrate its unified diversity were shattered in the fratricidal conflict that engulfed America.

Like many Americans, Whitman and his family daily checked the lists of wounded in the newspapers, and one day in December 1862 the family was jolted by the appearance of the name of "G. W. Whitmore" on the casualty roster from Fredericksburg. Fearful that the name was a garbled version of George Washington Whitman's, Walt immediately headed to Virginia to seek out his brother. Changing trains in Philadelphia, Whitman had his pocket picked on the crowded platform, and, penniless, he continued his journey to Washington, where, fortunately, he ran into William Douglas O'Connor, the writer and abolitionist he had met in Boston, who loaned him money. Futilely searching for George in the nearly forty Washington hospitals, Walt finally decided to take a government boat and army-controlled train to the battlefield at Fredericksburg to see if George was still there. After finding George's unit and discovering that his brother had received only a superficial facial wound, Whitman's relief turned to horror as he encountered a sight he would never forget: outside of a mansion converted into a field hospital, he came upon "a heap of amputated feet, legs, arms, hands, &c., a full load for a one-horse cart" (*PW*, 1:32). They were, he wrote in his journal, "human fragments, cut, bloody, black and blue, swelled and sickening" (*NUPM*, 2:504). Nearby were "several dead bodies . . . each cover'd with its brown woolen blanket" (*PW*, 1:32). The sight would continue to haunt this poet who had so confidently celebrated the physical body, who had claimed that the soul existed only *in* the body, that the arms and legs were extensions of the soul, the legs moving the soul through the world and the hands allowing the soul to express itself. Now a generation of young American males, the very males on whom he had staked the future of democracy, were literally being disarmed, amputated, killed. It was this amputation, this fragmenting of the Union – in both a literal and a figurative sense – that Whitman would address for the next few years, as he devoted himself to becoming the arms and legs of the wounded and maimed soldiers in the Civil War hospitals. By running errands for them, writing letters for them, encircling them in his arms, he tried, the best he could, to make them whole again.

This extraordinary hospital service, which took a tremendous toll on Whitman's own health as he spent countless long nights in the poorly ventilated wards, began spontaneously during his mission to George. He had fully anticipated that he would return to New York after determining that George was safe, but, after telegraphing his mother and the rest of the family that he had found George, he decided to stay with his brother for a few days. During this time he got to know the young soldiers, both Union and Confederate (he talked to a number of Southern prisoners of war). He assisted in the burial of the dead still lying on the bloody battlefield, where on December 13 there had been 18,000 Northern and Southern troops killed or wounded (and where, the next day, Robert E. Lee, sickened by the carnage, declined to attack General Ambrose Burnside's Union troops, even though they were in a vulnerable position).

Although Whitman had already written some of the poems that he would eventually publish in his Civil War book *Drum-Taps* (notably the "recruitment" poems like "Beat! Beat! Drums!" or "First O Songs for Prelude" that evoked the frightening yet exhilarating energy of cities arming for battle), it was only now, encountering the horrifying after-effects of a real battle, that the powerful Civil War poems began to emerge. In the journal he kept while at George's camp, Whitman

Figure 5 Photograph by Alexander Gardner, Washington, DC (1863?).
Courtesy Charles E. Feinberg Collection of Walt Whitman, Library of
Congress.

noted a "*Sight at daybreak* (in camp in front of the hospital tent) on a
stretcher, three dead men lying, each with a blanket spread over him
– I lift up one and look at the young man's face, calm and yellow. 'tis
strange! (Young man: I think this face, of yours the face of my dead

Christ!)" (*NUPM*, 2:513). As would be the case with many of the poems in *Drum-Taps*, this journal sketch gradually was transformed into a poem:

> A sight in camp in the day-break grey and dim,
> As from my tent I emerge so early, sleepless,
> As slow I walk in the cool fresh air, the path near by the hospital-tent,
> Three forms I see on stretchers lying, brought out there, untended lying,
> Over each the blanket spread, ample brownish woolen blanket,
> Grey and heavy blanket, folding, covering all.
> . . .
> Then to the third – a face nor child, nor old, very calm, as of beautiful yellow-white ivory;
> Young man, I think I know you – I think this face of yours is the face of the Christ himself;
> Dead and divine, and brother of all, and here again he lies. (*D-T*, 46)

The journal entry and poem offer a glimpse into how Whitman began restructuring his poetic project after the Civil War began. He was still writing a "new Bible" here, re-experiencing the Crucifixion in Fredericksburg. But this crucifixion does not redeem sinners and create an atonement with God so much as it posits divinity in everyone and mourns senseless loss: this one young man's death amidst the thousands is as significant as any in history. And, for Whitman, the massive slaughter of young soldier-Christs would create for all those who survived the war an obligation to construct a nation worthy of their great sacrifice. The America that he would write of after the Civil War would be a more chastened, less innocent nation, a nation that had gone through its baptism in blood and one that would from now on be tested against the stern measure of this bloodshed.

During the days he spent with George's unit, Whitman often went into the makeshift hospital outside of which he had seen the pile of amputated limbs. "I do not see that I do much good to these wounded and dying," he wrote; "but I cannot leave them" (*PW*, 1:33). As if to underscore his own attempts to hold the Union together, to reconcile rather than punish, to help love triumph over revenge, he found himself particularly attracted to a 19-year-old Confederate soldier from Mississippi, who had had a leg amputated. Whitman visited him regularly in the battlefield hospital and then continued to visit him when the soldier was transferred to a Washington hospital. "Our affection is quite an affair, quite romantic," he wrote (*Corr.*, 1:81). It wouldn't be the last intimacy he would experience with a Confederate soldier; at the end of the war, Whitman would enter the longest affectional relationship of his life with a former Confederate soldier named Peter Doyle, a friendship discussed later in this chapter. Something surprising – and perhaps unexpected even to Whitman – was happening to the "calamus" emotions that he had described in 1860; the intimate expressions of manly friendship now became generalized, perhaps sublimated, in the poet's many close relationships with injured soldiers over the next three years. Extant letters from these soldiers clearly indicate the intensity of the love that these young men felt for Whitman, and his letters to them demonstrate that the affection was reciprocated. The language of this correspondence is difficult to categorize – it is partly that of lovers, partly that of friends, partly that of son to father and father to son (many of the letters to Whitman are addressed to "Dear Father"), and partly that of calm, wise, old counselor to confused, scared, and half-literate young men.

We cannot be certain when Whitman made his decision to stay in Washington, DC. Like virtually all of the abrupt changes in his life, this one came with no planning, no advance notice, no preparation. He had gone to New Orleans on a similar spur-of-the-moment decision, just as he had suddenly quit teaching, just as he had packed up and gone to Boston, and just as he would years later decide overnight to settle in Camden, New Jersey. He was a profoundly *unsettled* person, who seemed able to shuck expected obligations and even relationships without much regret: he existed, as he said, on a kind of "Open Road": "The long brown path before me leading wherever I choose . . . I will scatter myself among men and women as I go":

> Allons! we must not stop here,
> However sweet these laid-up stores, however convenient this dwelling
>   we cannot remain here,
> However shelter'd this port and however calm these waters we must
>   not anchor here,
> However welcome the hospitality that surrounds us we are permitted
>   to receive it but a little while. (*LG*, 154)

One day Whitman simply left Brooklyn and New York and his family home to find his brother, and he never really came back.

Perhaps the decision was made while he was in the field hospital, nursing the wounded and developing his relationship with the young Mississippi soldier; it was then that he wrote to his mother and told her he might seek employment for a while in Washington, and it was then that he wrote to Emerson to ask for letters of recommendation to the secretary of state and the secretary of the treasury, who were both acquaintances of Emerson. But perhaps Whitman's decision was conclusively made on his trip back from Fredericksburg to Washington, right after a somber New Year's Day 1863, when – quickly earning the trust and respect of the doctors at the battlefield – he was put in charge of a trainload of casualties who had to be transferred to hospitals in the capital. While the wounded were being moved from a train to a steamboat for the trip up the Potomac, Whitman wandered among them, writing down their messages to their families, promising to send them, comforting the soldiers with his calm and concern. Perhaps by the time he got to Washington, determined to stay a few days in order to visit wounded soldiers from Brooklyn, he already knew at some level that he would have to remain there for the duration of the war.

His Boston connections were serving him well now; not only did he get letters of introduction from Emerson, but he got a room in the boarding house of William Douglas O'Connor and, through the efforts of Charles Eldridge – the publisher of the 1860 *Leaves*, who was now assistant to the army paymaster – he got a part-time job as a copyist in the paymaster's office. O'Connor and his wife Nellie provided Whitman his meals, and the poet began receiving contributions from his brother Jeff and others in Brooklyn who heard of his work in the hospitals. Whitman used what funds he had to buy small gifts for the wounded soldiers – candy and tobacco and flavored syrup and books – and he soon became a familiar figure in the hospitals. Prematurely gray and looking a decade or two older than his 43 years, Whitman must have seemed to the soldiers – many of whom were still in their teens – some sort of tattered Saint Nick, handing out treats and bringing good cheer. Many referred to him as "Old Man," and his presence was for some of the young men avuncular, for some paternal, and, for almost all, magical.

Whitman strove to exude a buoyant, healthy personality as he brought these men oranges, stamps and stationery, tobacco, small change, ice cream, friendship, and love. He visited the wards almost daily, often writing letters for the soldiers. In his visits to approximately 100,000 soldiers, his passionate devotion to young men – the "calamus" relationships we explored in the previous chapter – found a socially sanctioned outlet. He addressed himself to the emotional needs of soldiers while doctors worked (often with disastrous results) on soldiers' bodies. Given that pre-antiseptic medical intervention was as likely to cause infection as to heal, Whitman's ministrations were the more effective of the two. Several soldiers believed that he saved their lives. He had the full support of D. Willard Bliss, the chief surgeon at Armory Square Hospital, who testified later that "no one person who assisted in the hospitals during the war accomplished so much good to the soldier and for the Government as Mr. Whitman." Still, the poet's attachment to soldiers raised concerns in some quarters. Two women nurses, Harriet Foote Hawley and Amanda Akin, reacted to him in very negative ways, disliking his unorthodox beliefs and disapproving of his charged relationships with men (Murray 1996–7, 70–2).

Those critical of Whitman probably held that he promoted not a "beautiful and sane affection" but an unmanly manhood. This was certainly the conclusion of Thomas Wentworth Higginson, who, after the war, accused Whitman of evading his manly duty of military service and of embodying an "intermediate sex," neither man nor woman. Whitman's war work would come to color discussions of his poetry, his morality, and his overall reputation. For his defenders, such as William Douglas O'Connor, John Burroughs, and later Richard Maurice Bucke, Whitman's war work represented Christ-like efforts to restore life rather than destroy it. They recognized the male–male attachments at the heart of his work and his unconventional version of masculinity. John Burroughs, gesturing toward Whitman's complexity, speculated that "he was not an athlete, or a rough, but a great tender mother-man" (Barrus 1931, 339). The gender-role fluidity that was so bothersome to Higginson fascinated Burroughs and Bucke just as it did the soldiers in the hospitals.

To better support his hospital work, Whitman tried to exploit every connection he had in order to find a good job. The nation's capital was in a chaotic – even surreal – state in 1863, with unpaved, muddy streets and many half-built governmental edifices, including the Capitol building itself, with its vast new dome rising above the city, but still in only skeletal form. President Lincoln insisted that construction of the capital's buildings proceed at full pace, so, while the nation was tearing itself apart in civil war, the nation's capital was continuing to erect a unified and elegant governmental center, designed by the French architect Pierre L'Enfant. It was as if the capital had become a metaphor of the nation itself, half-built and in a struggle to determine whether it would end in fulfillment or destruction. Some of the newly constructed buildings almost immediately became hospitals, and when Whitman described the Civil War as turning the nation into a ward of casualties – America, "though only in her early youth," he wrote, was "already to hospital brought" – he no doubt had in mind the way the emerging governmental center of the country was being transformed into a vast hospital (*PW*, 2:378). The US Patent Office became a hospital in 1863, and Whitman noted the irony of the "rows of sick, badly wounded and dying soldiers" surrounding the "glass cases" displaying American inventions – guns and machines and other signs of progress (*PW*, 1:40). The wrecked bodies dispersed among the displays were what "progress" had brought, the result of new inventions that had created modern warfare. Washington was a noisy city during these years: the noise *in* the city was of construction; the noise just *outside* the city was of destruction; and the two activities conjoined in the dozens of makeshift Washington hospitals that held the shattered bodies of America's young men.

These were active and intense times for Whitman. In addition to his exhausting daily hospital rounds, he continued his job in the paymaster's office. This work usually took up only a few hours a day, though occasionally Whitman had to go on trips to visit troops, as when he traveled to Analostan Island in July of 1863 to help issue paychecks to the First Regiment US Colored Troops and was "well pleas'd" with their professional conduct and strong demeanor, as well as struck by the names of the black soldiers as the roll was called – George Washington, John Quincy Adams, Daniel Webster, James Madison, John Brown. The heritage of the nation, Whitman realized, was now being carried forward and fought for by a much more diverse citizenry; the African American soldiers, like Whitman's own brothers, bore the names of the nation's proud past. The war, for all of its destruction, was clearing the space for a broader American identity. Meanwhile, the news from Whitman's family was not good. His brother Andrew was extremely ill; his brother Jesse was increasingly violent (and even threatened his brother Jeff's young daughter); his sister Hannah was miserable in a disastrous marriage to an abusive husband;

and Whitman's mother wanted Walt home to help sort things out. Whitman did go back to New York for a visit toward the end of 1863 and saw Andrew for the last time; Andrew died at age 36, leaving behind two children and a pregnant, alcoholic wife, who later became a prostitute. The proliferating family problems were a deep concern to Whitman, but he nonetheless felt compelled to return to Washington and his soldier-friends there, to whom he wrote regularly during the weeks he was in New York.

Whitman came to know many people in Washington who would be important to him in the future: at the O'Connors' home, he met powerful Washington figures from political, literary, and social circles. One day while heading to the hospitals, he met John Burroughs, an aspiring young writer who, a couple of years previously, had started frequenting Pfaff's beerhall in New York in the hope of meeting Whitman, whose work he greatly admired. Now this chance encounter in Washington led to one of the most enduring friendships of Whitman's life; he spent most Sundays at the home of Burroughs and his wife Ursula, who also became one of Whitman's closest friends. Burroughs and O'Connor would both end up writing (with considerable help from Whitman himself) some of the earliest biographical treatments of the poet, and, despite some arguments with him over the years, both would remain unwavering supporters.

Whitman also met artists in Washington, like the photographer Alexander Gardner, who admired *Leaves of Grass* and who photographed Whitman frequently during the war years, recording the striking toll the war was taking on Whitman's appearance. The Gardner photographs show a tired, somber, yet very determined Whitman, who seemed to be absorbing not only soldiers' stories but their pain also. The war was taking a similar toll on many faces: often Whitman would watch Lincoln's carriage pass by, and he noted how the president "looks more careworn even than usual – his face with deep cut lines" (*Corr.*, 1:113). One day Whitman ran into another Boston acquaintance, the publisher James Redpath, who, impressed with the work Whitman was doing, organized a fund-raising campaign for the poet's hospital work. Redpath also considered (but finally decided against) publishing the sketches Whitman was writing about his war experiences, a book Whitman called *Memoranda During the War*. Redpath had published Louisa May Alcott's account of her Civil War nursing, *Hospital Sketches*, and Whitman was anxious to offer his own alternative version of nursing during the war. (He offered Redpath a volume that would be considerably more than "mere hospital sketches" and that would "ventilate my general democracy" [*Corr.*, 1:171].) Whitman's book, when it finally did appear as a self-published volume copyrighted in 1875, was composed of numerous short articles, many of which he had published in Brooklyn newspapers and in the *New York Times*, for whom he served as a kind of occasional Washington correspondent. These pieces would eventually form the heart of his autobiographical work, *Specimen Days*.

Walking the wards was for Whitman like walking America: every bed contained a representative of a different region, a different city or town, a different way of life. He loved the varied accents and the diverse physiognomies. "While I was with wounded and sick in thousands of cases from the New England States, and from New York, New Jersey, and Pennsylvania, and from Michigan, Wisconsin, Ohio, Indiana, Illinois, and all the Western States, I was with more or less from all the States, North and South, without exception" (*PW*, 1:113). His trip to New Orleans had taken him across a good part of the nation, but it was in the hospital wards that he *really* traveled the United States and crossed boundaries otherwise not easily passed: "I was with many rebel officers and men among our wounded, and gave them always what I had, and tried to cheer them the same as any . . . Among the black soldiers, wounded or sick, and in the contraband camps, I also took my way whenever in their neighborhood, and did what I could for them" (*PW*, 1:113–14). And with all those he met, he both sought and offered love: "What an attachment grows up between us, started from hospital cots, where pale young faces lie & wounded or sick bodies," he wrote; "The doctors tell me I supply the patients with a medicine which all their drugs & bottles & powders are helpless to yield" (*Corr.*, 1:122). He had become a physician after all, dispensing the medicine of hope and affection, the same medicine he hoped would heal a country, suture its wounds, repair its fracture. And he sought to dispense this medicine not only to soldiers on his hospital visits but to all Americans through his books.

During all the time of his hospital service, Whitman was writing poems, a new kind of poem for him, poems about the war experience, but almost never about battles – rather about the after-effects of warfare: the moonlight illuminating the dead on the battlefields, the churches turned into hospitals, the experience of dressing wounds, the encounter with a dead enemy in a coffin, the trauma of battle nightmares for soldiers who had returned home. He gathered these poems along with the few he had written just before the war (the ones that Thayer and Eldridge had originally planned to publish as *Banner at Day-Break*) and worked on combining them in a book called *Drum-Taps*, the title evoking both the beating of the drums that accompanied soldiers into battle and the beating out of "Taps," the death march sounded at the burial of soldiers (originally played on the drum instead of the bugle). After the burst of creativity in the mid- and late 1850s that resulted in the vastly expanded 1860 *Leaves*, Whitman had not written many poems until he got to Washington, where the daily encounters with soldiers opened a fresh vein of creativity, resulting in a poetry more modest in ambition and more muted in its claims, a poetry in which death was no longer something indistinguishable from life ("Has any one supposed it lucky to be born?" Whitman had written in "Song of Myself"; "I hasten to inform him or her it is just as lucky to die, and I know it") but rather now revealed itself as something horrifying, grotesque, and omnipresent. The poems were so different from any that had appeared in *Leaves*, in fact, that Whitman originally assumed they could not be joined in the same book with those earlier poems. It would be a long, slow process that would eventually allow the absorption of *Drum-Taps* into *Leaves of Grass*.

As the war entered its final year, Whitman was facing physical and emotional exhaustion. Eighteen sixty-four began with one of his closest soldier-friends, Lewis Brown (with whom he had imagined living after the war was over), having his leg amputated; Whitman watched the operation through a window at Armory Square Hospital. In February and March, he traveled to the Virginia battlefront to nurse soldiers in field hospitals, then in April he stood for three hours watching General Burnside's troops march through Washington, until Whitman could pick out his brother George. He marched with George and gave him news from home. It would be the last time Whitman would see his brother before George was captured by Confederate troops after a battle in the fall. During the early summer, Whitman began to complain of a sore throat, dizziness, and a "bad feeling" in his head. Physician friends urged him to check into one of the hospitals he had been visiting, and they finally convinced him to go back to New York for a rest. He took his manuscript of *Drum-Taps* with him to

Brooklyn, hoping to publish it himself while he was there. Soon after he left Washington, the capital was attacked by the Confederates and many thought it was about to be captured; he missed the most terrifying months of the war in the District of Columbia.

In Brooklyn, Whitman could not stop doing what had now become both a routine and a reason for his existence: he visited wounded soldiers in New York-area hospitals. But he also re-established contacts with old friends from the Pfaff's beerhall days, and he explored some new beer saloons with them. He wrote some more articles for the *New York Times* and other papers, and he took care of pressing family matters, including the commitment of his increasingly unstable brother Jesse to the Kings County Lunatic Asylum (where he would die six years later). The year ended with the arrival at the family home of George's personal items, including his war diary, which Whitman presumably read at this time. Though Whitman did not then know it, George had been sent to the Libby Prison in Richmond, Virginia, and would also serve time in military prisons in Salisbury, North Carolina, and finally in Danville, Virginia. In the hope of effecting George's release, Whitman began a campaign, in both newspaper articles and letters to government officials, to support a general exchange of prisoners between the Confederacy and the Union, something Union generals tended to oppose because they believed such an exchange would benefit the South by returning troops to an army in desperate need of more men.

By the beginning of 1865, Whitman was very anxious to return to Washington, which he now considered to be his home. Friends there had been working on getting him a better government position, and O'Connor helped arrange a clerkship in the Indian Bureau of the Department of the Interior. Whitman carried his *Drum-Taps* manuscript back to Washington, hoping that his increased income might allow him to publish the book. He moved to a new apartment, run by what he called a "secesh" (or Southern-sympathizing) landlady, and he began work in the Indian Bureau; his desk was in the US Patent Office Building, which he had been visiting when it was used as a temporary hospital. As a clerk there, he met delegations of various Indian tribes from the West, and, just as he had come to know the geographical range of America through his hospital visits, so now he gained direct experience with Native Americans. He had included Indians in his poems of America, cataloguing "the red aborigines" in "Starting from

Paumanok," for example, celebrating the way they "charg[ed] the water and the land with names" (thus he always preferred the name "Paumanok" to "Long Island" and often argued that aboriginal names for American places were always superior to names imported from Europe). The impact of his experiences at the Indian Bureau is apparent in such later poems as "Osceola" and "Yonnondio," memorializing the native cultures that were, he believed, inevitably disappearing.

George Whitman was released from Danville prison in February and returned to the family home in Brooklyn in March. Whitman got a furlough from the Indian Bureau so that he could go see George, and, while in Brooklyn, Whitman arranged with a New York printer for the publication of *Drum-Taps*. He signed a contract on April 1, and then, eight days later, while he was still in Brooklyn, the Civil War ended, with General Lee surrendering at Appomattox; five days after that, President Lincoln was assassinated at Ford's Theatre in Washington. It is ironic that Whitman, who spent most of the final two years of the war in the capital, was not there for its most traumatic and memorable events: he was back in New York during the main Confederate assault on Washington, and he was in New York again when the capital celebrated the end of the war and then mourned the loss of the president.

But the fact that Whitman was at his mother's home in Brooklyn led to one of his greatest poems, because he heard the news about Lincoln that April morning when the lilac bushes were blooming in his mother's dooryard, where he went to console himself and where he inhaled the scent of the lilacs, which became for him viscerally bound to the memory of Lincoln's death. He began writing his powerful elegy to Lincoln, "When Lilacs Last in the Dooryard Bloom'd," after *Drum-Taps* had already been delivered to the printer. He was able quickly to add to *Drum-Taps*, before the book was set in type, a brief poem about Lincoln's death, "Hush'd Be the Camps To-day," but his "Lilacs" elegy and his uncharacteristically rhymed and metered elegy for Lincoln, "O Captain! My Captain!," were written after the book was in press. Whitman therefore compiled a *Sequel to Drum-Taps* and had it printed up when he went back to Washington. In October he returned to Brooklyn to oversee the collating and binding of *Sequel* with *Drum-Taps*. He subtitled *Sequel* "When Lilacs Last in the Dooryard Bloom'd and Other Pieces," and the very title registered the fragmentation that now characterized his poetry and his nation, shattered and in pieces (in "Lilacs," he described the "debris and debris" of the war's casualties and of the nation's current condition). He dated the *Sequel* 1865–6, offering another significantly hyphenated moment. Just as his 1860–1 *Leaves* marked the division between a nation at peace and a nation rent by war, so now did the sequel mark the reunification, a country moving from a year of war to the difficult first year of its reunified peace, from the horror of disintegration to the challenge of reconstruction.

In joining *Drum-Taps* and *Sequel*, Whitman created a book whose physical form echoed the challenges the postwar nation was facing as it entered the stormy period of Reconstruction. Whitman, too, was entering a period of poetic reconstruction, searching for ways to absorb the personal and national trauma of the Civil War into *Leaves of Grass*. As soon as the war ended, he began to realize that the nation's hopes and history had to be reunified and that his original goals for *Leaves of Grass* – to project an optimistic democratic future for America – should not be abandoned but rather had to be integrated with the trauma of the Civil War. He faced the difficult task now of reopening *Leaves of Grass* to find a way to absorb into his growing book the horror of the nation's fratricidal war.

His life was undergoing many changes in the weeks and months following the end of the war. One major event happened unexpectedly: on a stormy night, while riding the streetcar home after dinner at John and Ursula Burroughs' apartment, Whitman began talking with the conductor, a 21-year-old Irish immigrant and former Confederate soldier named Peter Doyle. Doyle later recalled that Whitman was the only passenger, and "we were familiar at once – I put my hand on his knee – we understood." "From that time on," Doyle recalled, "we were the biggest sort of friends" (Bucke 1897, 23). It would be a friendship that would last for the rest of Whitman's life, and it was the most intense and romantic friendship the poet would have. Like Whitman, Doyle came from a large family, and Walt got to know Doyle's widowed mother and his siblings well; they came to be a second family for him. Whitman continued visiting soldiers in Washington hospitals during the first years following the war, as the number of hospitals gradually decreased and only the most difficult cases remained, but he now focused his attention increasingly on this single young former artilleryman from the South. Like so many of Whitman's closest friends, Doyle had only a rudimentary education and was from the working class. These young men were reflections of Whitman's own youthful self, and he saw his poetry as speaking for them, putting into words what they could not, becoming the vocalization of the common man, without aristocratic airs, without elite schooling, without the weary formalities of tradition. For Whitman, then, Doyle represented America's future: healthy, witty, handsome, good-humored, hard-working, enamored of good times, he gave Whitman's life some energy and hope during an otherwise bleak time. They rode the streetcars together, drank at the Union Hotel bar, took long walks outside the city, and quoted poetry to each other (Whitman recited Shakespeare, Doyle limericks). As Whitman's health continued to deteriorate in the late 1860s and early 1870s, the young former soldier nursed the aging former nurse and offered comfort to the poet just as Walt had to so many sick soldiers. And just as Whitman had picked up the germs of many of his poems from the stories soldiers had told him, so now he picked up from Doyle – who had been at Ford's Theatre the night John Wilkes Booth shot the president – the narrative of the assassination of Lincoln that he would use for the Lincoln lectures that he would deliver regularly in his later years.

Only in 1870 did the Doyle–Whitman relationship encounter severe problems. In some of the most intriguing and often-discussed entries in all of Whitman's notebooks, the poet records a cryptic resolution: "TO GIVE UP ABSOLUTELY *& for good, from the present hour, this* FEVERISH, FLUCTUATING, *useless* UNDIGNIFIED PURSUIT *of 16.4 – too long, (much too long)* persevered in, – so humiliating" (*NUPM*, 2:888). Critics eventually broke Whitman's numeric/alphabetic code (16 = P; 4 = D) and realized that he was writing about his relationship with Doyle. Whitman goes on to urge himself to "Depress the adhesive nature / It is in excess – making life a torment / Ah this diseased, feverish disproportionate adhesiveness / Remember Fred Vaughan" (*NUPM*, 2:889–90). Vaughan, the close friend who probably inspired Whitman's "Calamus" poems, shared many traits with Doyle, and Whitman came to be jealous of both men when they did not return his love with the fervor he demanded. Soon after Whitman had met Doyle, he revised his "Calamus" sequence and removed the darker poems that expressed despair at being abandoned. But in 1870, those same dark emotions reappeared, though somehow this time Whitman and his partner managed to work their way through the trouble. They never lived together, though Walt dreamed of doing so, and, while their relationship would never regain the intensity it had in the mid-1860s, Doyle and Whitman continued to correspond, and Doyle visited Whitman regularly for the next two decades after the poet moved to Camden, New Jersey.

Just when Whitman was feeling secure in his government employment, all hell broke loose. In May, 1865, a new secretary of the interior, James Harlan of Iowa, was sworn in and immediately set out to clean up his department, issuing a directive to abolish non-essential positions and to dismiss any employee whose "moral character" was questionable. Harlan was a formidable figure – a former US Senator, Methodist minister, and president of Iowa Wesleyan College – and, when he saw Whitman's working copy of the 1860 *Leaves of Grass* (which the poet kept in his desk so that he could revise his poems during slow times at the office), he was appalled. On June 20, Whitman (along with a number of other Interior Department employees) received a dismissal notice. He quickly turned to his fiery friend O'Connor, who at that time worked in the Treasury Department. O'Connor, at some risk to his own career, took immediate action: he contacted the assistant attorney general, J. Hubley Ashton, who in turn talked with Harlan, only to find that not only was Harlan dead set against rescinding the dismissal order, he was ready to prevent Whitman from getting work in any other governmental agency. Ashton talked Harlan out of interfering with Whitman's appointment outside of the Interior Department, and then he convinced attorney general James Speed to hire Whitman in his office. Whitman became a clerk in that office the next day, liked the work better (he aided in the preparation of requests for pardons from Confederates and later copied documents for delivery to the president and cabinet members), and held the job until 1874, when he forfeited it because of ill health.

The whole flap over Whitman's firing seemed to be over in a day, but O'Connor, a highly regarded editor, novelist, and journalist as well as a governmental servant, could not control his rage at Harlan and began to write a diatribe against the moralistic secretary of the interior and his "commission of an outrage" – the unceremonious dumping of Walt Whitman, *"the Kosmical man – . . . the* ADAMUS *of the nineteenth century – not an individual, but* MANKIND" (Loving 1978, 171). O'Connor went on for nearly fifty pages, excoriating Harlan and sanctifying Whitman, offering a ringing endorsement of the poet's work and his life, emphasizing his hospital work and his love of country, and locating any indecency in Harlan's "horrible inanity of prudery," not in the poetry itself (Loving 1978, 191). Whitman offered O'Connor advice and suggestions on the piece, which O'Connor titled "The Good Gray Poet," creating an epithet that would attach itself to Whitman from then on. The pamphlet was published at the beginning of 1866 and had a major impact on the changing public perception of Whitman: though O'Connor did not downplay Whitman's frankness about the body, in his hands the transformation had begun from outrageous, immoral, indiscriminate, and radical poet of sex to saint-like, impoverished, aging poet of strong American values.

Around this time, Whitman visited George Washington's home in Mount Vernon, perhaps looking for some stable point in a national history that now seemed to be spinning out of control. That pile of body parts he had seen when he first went to Fredericksburg to search for his brother had expanded almost infinitely during the years of the war. There was now a new stubborn reality he would have to learn to incorporate in his radically altered post-1860 poetry: instead of absorbing an ameliorative, evolving, progressive, expanding self and nation and cosmos into his affirmative song, he would begin cataloging mass death. This grisly catalog would eventually expand to over 600,000 deaths (projected as a percentage of the nation's population, we'd be talking about nearly seven million dead young men today).

We can find pieces of this dark catalog throughout Whitman's wartime poetry, but perhaps never so effectively as in his prose *Memoranda During the War*, where he writes the longest sentence he would ever compose, inventing a syntax of mass death, an utterance that wanders the ruined nation to gather up "the infinite dead," pausing again and again to absorb the horror, the details, the unimaginable numbers of dead young men whose bodies eluded the grave and were composed back into the landscape itself. The sentence buries seven parenthetical insertions among its thirty-some dashes, creating a jagged syntactical field. And this astonishing catalog of a sentence ends up, after its nearly 400 words, being a sentence *fragment*. There is no way, Whitman discovered, to predicate *this* subject: "The dead in this war." These numberless dead are of course beyond animation, themselves now fragments of bodies, amputated selves, irretrievable, that have so "saturated" America's land that we the living are now fated to reap forevermore a harvest of death, with blood in every grain we eat:

The dead in this war – there they lie, strewing the fields and woods
and valleys and battle-fields of the south – Virginia, the Peninsula –
Malvern hill and Fair Oaks – the banks of the Chickahominy – the
terraces of Fredericksburgh – Antietam bridge – the grisly ravines of
Manassas – the bloody promenade of the Wilderness – the varieties
of the *strayed* dead, (the estimate of the War department is 25,000
national soldiers kill'd in battle and never buried at all, 5,000 drown'd
– 15,000 inhumed by strangers, or on the march in haste, in hitherto
unfound localities – 2,000 graves cover'd by sand and mud by Mississippi
freshets, 3,000 carried away by caving-in of banks, &c.,) – Gettysburgh,
the West, Southwest – Vicksburgh – Chattanooga – the trenches of
Petersburgh – the numberless battles, camps, hospitals everywhere –
the crop reap'd by the mighty reapers, typhoid, dysentery, inflammations
– and blackest and loathesomest of all, the dead and living burial-pits,
the prison-pens of Andersonville, Salisbury, Belle-Isle, &c., (not Dante's
pictured hell and all its woes, its degradations, filthy torments, excell'd
those prisons) – the dead, the dead, the dead – *our* dead – or South
or North, ours all, (all, all, all, finally dear to me) – or East or West –
Atlantic coast or Mississippi valley – somewhere they crawl'd to die,
alone, in bushes, low gullies, or on the sides of hills – (there, in secluded
spots, their skeletons, bleach'd bones, tufts of hair, buttons, fragments
of clothing, are occasionally found yet) – our young men once so
handsome and so joyous, taken from us – the son from the mother, the
husband from the wife, the dear friend from the dear friend – the
clusters of camp graves, in Georgia, the Carolinas, and in Tennessee –
the single graves left in the woods or by the road-side, (hundreds,
thousands, obliterated) – the corpses floated down the rivers, and caught
and lodged, (dozens, scores, floated down the upper Potomac, after the
cavalry engagements, the pursuit of Lee, following Gettysburgh) – some
lie at the bottom of the sea – the general million, and the special
cemeteries in almost all the States – the infinite dead – (the land entire
saturated, perfumed with their impalpable ashes' exhalation in Nature's
chemistry distill'd, and shall be so forever, in every future grain of
wheat and ear of corn, and every flower that grows, and every breath we
draw) – not only Northern dead leavening Southern soil – thousands,
aye tens of thousands, of Southerners, crumble to-day in Northern
earth. (*PW*, 1:114–15)

Whitman entitled this section of his *Memoranda* "The Million Dead,
Too, Summ'd Up," using his characteristic contraction-apostrophe,
which here creates a haunting ambiguity, because the sentence with
all its embedded statistics, its death-data, does give us the Civil War

dead *summed up*, but the contraction also invites us to fill in a few more letters, as we realize this death sentence literally *summons up* the dead, reminding us of their physical presence throughout the landscape, North and South, and insisting on their physical emergence in everything that grows from the soil they dissolved into. Whitman's catalog is a summing and a summoning, and the summons is not just of the dead but also of the living, who are being summoned to witness this mass death and, grotesque as it may seem, *ingest* it, live off of it, make a future out of it. Making a future out of that landscape of death would be Whitman's challenge for the rest of his life, as he tried to generate a nation worthy of such sacrifice. His old idea of "compost" was cast into a national process: the country had to create new life out of the decomposing bodies of a generation of its young men.

Everywhere, America was being redefined, and Whitman was now searching for hints, answers, suggestions, about America's future. He attended baseball games; the new sport was quickly becoming the national game after returning Civil War soldiers, who had learned to play it in military camps, began organizing teams in various parts of the country. Whitman would be the first to call it "America's game," with the "snap, go, fling, of the American atmosphere." Maybe this unifying sport could help give the country a single identity again: he said the game was as important to "the sum total of our historic life" as our laws and Constitution. And he worked on *Leaves of Grass*, revising his 1860 edition incessantly (he still had the marked-up copy that Harlan had found in his desk), looking for a way that his book could continue to develop as an organizing force of American identity. By 1866, almost in desperation, Whitman felt it was imperative that he issue the first postwar edition of *Leaves*.

CHAPTER 6

Reconstructing *Leaves* of *Grass*, Restructuring a Life

In August and September of 1866, Whitman took time off from his job to go to New York and arrange for the printing of a new edition of *Leaves*. While there, he experienced the quickly changing and vastly expanding New York City – he wandered Central Park, took boat rides, and rekindled friendships with his stage-driver and ferryboat-worker friends, and he oversaw the typesetting of his new *Leaves*, which finally appeared near the end of the year, even though the title page dated the book 1867.

The 1867 *Leaves of Grass* is the most carelessly printed and the most chaotic of all the editions. Whitman had problems with the typesetters, whose work was filled with errors. He bound the book in five distinct formats, some with only the new edition of *Leaves of Grass*, some with *Leaves* plus *Drum-Taps*, some with *Leaves*, *Drum-Taps*, and *Sequel to Drum-Taps*, some with all of these along with another new cluster called *Songs Before Parting*, and some with only *Leaves* and *Songs Before Parting*. He was obviously confused about what form his book should take. He always believed that the history of *Leaves* paralleled the history of himself, and that both histories embodied the history of America in the nineteenth century, so we can read the 1867 edition as Whitman's first tentative attempt to absorb the Civil War into his book. By literally sewing the printed pages of *Drum-Taps* and *Sequel* into the back of some of the issues, he creates a jarring textual effect, as pagination and font fracture while he adds his poems of war and division to his earlier poems of absorption and nondiscrimination. The Union has been preserved, but this stripped and undecorated volume – the only edition of *Leaves* to contain no portrait of the poet

– manifests a kind of forced reconciliation, a recognition that everything now has to be reconfigured. *Leaves of Grass*, like the nation, was now entering a long period of reconstruction, one marked for Whitman by significantly reduced poetic activity. The poet now began to devote his energies to what would become a 15-year process of arranging and rearranging his poems in order to restructure the overall pattern of his book.

Whitman would keep shuffling, pruning, and adding to *Leaves* in order to try to solve the structural problems so evident in the 1867 edition. By 1870, *Leaves* took a radically new shape when the fifth edition appeared (known as the 1871–2 edition because of the varying dates on the title page, but actually first printed in 1870). This complex edition, which, like the 1867, appeared in several versions with different-colored covers, reveals Whitman's attempt to fully absorb the Civil War and its aftermath into his book, as the *Drum-Taps* poems are given their own "cluster" but also are scattered into other parts of *Leaves*, as the war experience bleeds out into the rest of the poems in sometimes subtle small additions and changes. This edition contains some revealing clusters of poems that appear here and then disappear in the much better-known 1881 arrangement; in the 1871–2 edition, "Marches now the War is Over" and "Songs of Insurrection" are two clusters that capture the charged historical moment of Reconstruction that this edition responds to.

In the development from the 1867 *Leaves* to the better integrated 1871–2 *Leaves*, Whitman was aided by the intervening efforts of the English writer William Michael Rossetti, who edited *Poems by Walt Whitman* (1868), the first British edition of Whitman's work. Rossetti's careful arrangement of the poems helped Whitman see new possibilities in his work, specifically how *Drum-Taps* could be integrated into the larger project of *Leaves of Grass*. Rossetti believed, however, that Whitman's work had to be expurgated for the sensibilities of British readers, and, as the English edition progressed, Whitman took various positions on Rossetti's suggestions for censoring, once seeming to grant permission (through his friend Moncure Conway) to substitute words for "father-stuff" and "onanist," but later telling Rossetti that "I cannot and will not consent, of my own volition, to countenance an expurgated edition of my pieces." Rossetti's diplomatic approach was to alter no words in Whitman's poems (though he often changed titles). Instead, if a poem might offend too many readers or provoke censors, he omitted it altogether. Rossetti regarded Whitman as one of the great poets of the English language and hoped that this selection of poems would augur a complete printing in England. *Poems by Walt Whitman*, reprinting approximately half of the 1867 *Leaves of Grass*, was critical for Whitman, since it made him English friends who later would help sustain him financially and who would advance his reputation on both sides of the Atlantic.

In 1870 Whitman published *Democratic Vistas* and *Passage to India* (both works carried the date 1871 on their title pages). *Passage to India*, a volume of 75 poems, one-third of them new, was intended as a follow-up volume to *Leaves of Grass*, one that would inaugurate a new emphasis in Whitman's poetry on the "unseen soul" and would thus complement his earlier songs of the "body and existence" (*PW*, 2:466). (He eventually curtailed the plan, in part because of poor health and in part because of his recurring realization that *Leaves of Grass* could absorb everything and that *Passage* – just like *Drum-Taps* earlier – could become part of the single large book.)

The title poem, "Passage to India," moves from the material to the spiritual. Much of the poem celebrates the highly publicized work of engineers, especially the suggestive global linking accomplished by the transcontinental railroad, the Suez Canal, and the Atlantic cable. (Whitman's enthusiasm for engineering accomplishments was magnified because of his pride in his brother Jeff, who had moved west in 1867 to become chief engineer charged with building and overseeing waterworks for St Louis – a "great work – a noble position," Walt exclaimed [*PW*, 1:326].) For Whitman, modern material accomplishments were most important as means to better understand the "aged fierce enigmas" (*LG*, 420) at the heart of spiritual questions. "Passage to India" is grand in conception and has had many admirers, but the poem's rhetorical excesses – apparent even in its heavy reliance on exclamation marks – reveal a poet not so much at odds with his subject matter as flagging in inspiration.

Whitman's celebration of engineers, architects, and machinists in "Passage to India" no doubt prompted the organizers of the 1871 exposition of the American Institute (a large industrial fair) to invite him to deliver the opening poem. Whitman accepted, glad of the $100 payment and the publicity that would follow from distribution of a pamphlet through Roberts Brothers, a Boston publisher. Assured publicity was welcome because his recent work had garnered few reviews. He hoped to benefit fully, and he prepared copies of his poem, "After All Not to Create Only" (later called "Song of the Exposition"), for release to the New York dailies. Reports on the effectiveness of Whitman's reading were mixed: some accounts indicated that the poet could not be heard over the workmen constructing exhibits, while other reports described a "good elocutionist" greeted by long applause. However, there was enough sarcasm in the press reports to make the event less than a thoroughgoing success.

If "Passage to India" and "After All Not to Create Only" were celebratory (perhaps at times naively so), *Democratic Vistas* mounted sustained criticism of Reconstruction-era failures. Based in part on essays that had appeared in the New York journal the *Galaxy* in 1867 and 1868, *Democratic Vistas* responds most immediately to a racist diatribe by the Scottish essayist and historian Thomas Carlyle, "Shooting Niagara: And After?" Carlyle's "great man" view of history left him impatient with democracy and opposed to efforts to expand the franchise in either the US or Britain. For him, the folly of giving the vote to blacks was akin to going over Niagara Falls in a barrel. Whitman grants Carlyle some general points, acknowledging, for example, the "appalling dangers of universal suffrage in the U.S." because of the "people's crudeness, vices, caprices." In fact, Whitman gazes piercingly at a society "canker'd, crude, superstitious and rotten," in which the "depravity of our business classes . . . is not less than has been supposed, but infinitely greater." Yet he contrasts these current problems with "democracy's convictions [and] aspirations" and ultimately provides a ringing endorsement of democracy as the safest and only legitimate course for the US. His thought on the intertwined fates of the US and democracy – his "convertible terms" – is future-oriented. He preceded the philosopher and educator John Dewey in arguing that the United States was not yet made and thus could not be categorically assessed, just as the history of democracy was yet to be written because "that history has yet to be enacted." "We have frequently printed the word Democracy," Whitman wrote in *Democratic Vistas*; "Yet I cannot too often repeat that it is a word the real gist of which still sleeps, quite unawaken'd" (*PW*, 2:390). Democracy always remained for Whitman an ideal goal, "resid[ing] altogether in the future" (*PW*, 2:390), and never a realized practice. The history of America, so he hoped, would eventually define the word for the first time, because in his own day, he believed, democracy was only "in its embryo condition" (*PW*, 2:392).

Crucial to his program for strengthening democracy are what he calls "personalism" (a form of individualism in which every person develops uniquely but always remains aware of his or her interconnectedness with the larger social body) and the nurturance of an appropriate "New World literature" that would demand more aggressive reading habits, literature that would awaken the populace and make them argue with the author instead of lull them to sleep and have them passively accept whatever the author professed.

For all of the idealism of *Democratic Vistas*, however, the work clearly arose out of Whitman's struggle with the radical politics of the Reconstruction era, and it raises troubling and perhaps unanswerable questions about his attitudes toward the Radical Republican agenda of quickly securing civil rights and voting rights for freed (male) slaves. If Whitman's faith in the future of American democracy was clear, his vision of the place of African Americans in that future was blurred. As he was writing *Democratic Vistas*, the shape of the new nation was uncertain, as malleable as the intense debates and shifting votes of a Congress that was revising the very Constitution and threatening to impeach the president, Andrew Johnson. Whitman, during this time, continued to spend evenings visiting the Civil War hospitals that remained opened, still filled with wounded soldiers two years after the war had ended, but he also devoted some of his time to trips to the Capitol to watch the extraordinary night sessions with their impassioned debates on Reconstruction legislation, including the Fourteenth and Fifteenth Amendments to the Constitution. For the Radical Republicans who controlled Congress, the war increasingly seemed to have been fought not just to emancipate the slaves (the Thirteenth Amendment had taken care of that) but to enfranchise them and guarantee them equal rights under the Constitution (this was the arena of the Fourteenth and Fifteenth Amendments, and the amazing debates dealt with the very tricky issue of trying to unwrite the Constitutional provision that slaves counted as only three-fifths of a person, and trying to inscribe just what the black person's newly granted full humanity meant). Whitman, like many Americans, was unsure about where he stood on these momentous issues.

While attending the debates, he looked at the racially changed world about him: "We had the greatest black procession here last Thursday – I didn't think there was so many darkeys, (especially wenches,) in the world – it was the anniversary of emancipation in this District"

(*Corr.*, 1:273–4). After blacks exercised their newly won right to vote in the District of Columbia, his fear intensified to alarm:

> We had the strangest procession here last Tuesday night, about 3000 darkeys, old & young, men & women – I saw them all – they turned out in honor of *their* victory in electing the Mayor, Mr. Bowen – the men were all armed with clubs or pistols – besides the procession in the street, there was a string went along the sidewalk in single file with bludgeons & sticks, yelling & gesticulating like madmen – it was quite comical, yet very disgusting & alarming in some respects – They were very insolent, & altogether it was a strange sight – they looked like so many wild brutes let loose – thousands of slaves from the Southern plantations have crowded up here – many are supported by the Gov't. (*Corr.*, 2:34–5).

As Whitman, like much of the nation, was reconstructing the rationale for the Civil War, he was also reconstructing his view of the place of black Americans in the life of the nation.

It is surprising that Whitman did not include any sustained reference to slaves and slavery in his original *Drum-Taps* poems, where he never raises the question of the place of the freed slaves in American culture. Soon after the war, however, he had begun asking some troubled questions: "Did the vast mass of the blacks, in Slavery in the United States, present a terrible and deeply complicated problem through the just ending century? But how if the mass of the blacks in freedom in the U.S. all through the ensuing century, should present a yet more terrible and deeply complicated problem?" (*PW*, 1:326). Whitman, before the war, was far more settled on the question of slavery than he was after the war on the question of African American citizenship. Before the war, he had been for freedom for the slaves; after the war, the very nature of that freedom became a problem for him.

This is the question that haunts *Democratic Vistas* and stands silently behind it. It is Whitman's ambivalence about the place of blacks in America's future that prevents him from ever issuing the firm rejoinder to Carlyle's "Shooting Niagara" (and its ugly "Nigger Question") that he had originally planned. He begins *Democratic Vistas* saying he will not "gloss over" the issue of universal suffrage, but that is exactly what he does: he discusses equality between the sexes, but after obliquely raising the issues of race in the opening pages, the essay veers away, never to return, except in some small-print notes at the end, notes that he did not republish with *Democratic Vistas* after the initial printing. In one manuscript fragment of what appear to be notes for a section of *Democratic Vistas* that he never wrote, he offers a kind of Darwinian view of race, saying "the blacks must either filter through in time or gradually eliminate & disappear, which is most likely though that termination is far off, or else must so develop in mental and moral qualities and in all the attributes of a leading and dominant race, (which I do not think likely)" (Price 1985, 205). Here Whitman sounds much like Carlyle, predicting the same eventual disappearance of the black race (such applications of evolutionary theory to the prophecy that the Negro race was destined to disappear were common in the postwar years), and expressing some contempt for the notion that the black race could progress enough to hold an equal place in American society.

Whitman's hesitancy to embrace the notion of a new American culture in which different races would share rights and power led in 1872 to a violent argument with his friend O'Connor, who could not believe that Whitman, of all people, would not endorse immediate black suffrage. While the specifics of the argument are shrouded in mystery, the bitterness led to a breakup of this important friendship, though O'Connor would later write passionately once again in defense of Whitman when his book was attacked by government authorities (see chapter 7).

Whitman's steady routine of life – mixing work as a Washington clerk with his ongoing literary projects – was fundamentally altered when a series of blows turned 1873 into one of the worst years in his life. On January 23, he suffered a stroke; in February his sister-in-law Mattie (wife of his brother Jeff) died of cancer; in May his beloved mother began to fail. Whitman – partially paralyzed, with weakness in his left leg and arm – managed to travel to Camden, New Jersey, arriving three days before his mother's death. He returned to Washington at the beginning of June, hoping to resume his job. But by the middle of the month he was back in Camden to stay, a partial invalid, moving into a working-class neighborhood with his brother George (a pipe inspector) and George's wife, Lou.

One can glimpse Whitman's emotional state in "Prayer of Columbus" (*Harper's Magazine*, March, 1874), which depicts Columbus – a mask of Whitman himself – as a battered, wrecked, paralyzed, old man, misunderstood in his own time. Gradually, however, the poet's spirits improved as he warmed to Camden and found ways to turn a dreary, struggling town into a supportive social environment. Among Camden's advantages was its proximity to Philadelphia, a city with a thriving intellectual and artistic community. Thomas Eakins, from his base at the Pennsylvania Academy of the Fine Arts, made Whitman the subject of a memorable portrait and numerous photographs, and he produced other work, including *Swimming*, informed by Whitman's vision. Whitman's interest in photography found a supportive milieu in Philadelphia, home of the country's oldest photographic society and host city for the journal *Philadelphia Photographer*. In addition, the University of Pennsylvania was quick to invite Eadweard Muybridge to continue his locomotion studies shortly after his first successful experiments in cinematic photography in 1884. Whitman absorbed the air of this excitement, even as he was extending his own experiment of incorporating photography directly into his literary project by including photos of himself in his new editions of *Leaves of Grass*.

Throughout the Camden years, despite his physical decline, the poet published steadily. Not long after his stroke, for example, he expanded and reworked his Civil War journalism and notebook entries and composed *Memoranda During the War* (1875–6). The book was published at the end of Reconstruction, when a rise in immigration and racial conflict strained national cohesion, and, to Whitman's mind, lent urgency once again to his argument that affectionate bonds between men constituted the vital core of American democracy. The prose in this volume is taut, concise, detailed, and unflinching. Although the Civil War received more press coverage than any previous war, Whitman worried that its true import would be lost, that what he called "the real war" would never be remembered. He lamented the lack of attention to the common soldiers and to the fortitude and love he had seen in his many visits with soldiers in the hospitals.

The nation's hundredth birthday, however, seemed to revive Whitman: *Memoranda* and his other centennial publications helped him recover from his most demoralized state. He had hoped to be asked to write the national hymn by the Centennial Commission (five others were asked before Bayard Taylor accepted), but the nation's centennial in fact passed by with little recognition of Whitman. He did not spend much time at the centennial fair held in Philadelphia just across the river from Camden. But he managed to create his own celebration of the centennial by bringing forth the variously labeled

"Author's Edition" or "Centennial Edition" of *Leaves of Grass.* The 1876 "edition" was technically a reissue of the 1871–2 *Leaves* with intercalations; he pasted four new poems on blank sections of pages, added an epigraph-poem that he personally signed, and included two "portraits," the old Hollyer engraving he had used as his 1855 frontispiece (reproduced above as figure 4) and a new engraving by William Linton of a recently taken photograph. Handsomely bound and proudly affiliating itself with the centennial, this version of *Leaves of Grass* emphasized Whitman's faith in the unity of his book with his country.

Whitman published a companion volume to this issue of *Leaves of Grass*, called *Two Rivulets* (1876), that gathered his Reconstruction writings and presented them in a highly experimental way: in one section he printed poetry on the top half and prose on the bottom half of each page. *Leaves of Grass* and *Two Rivulets* (which incorporated *Memoranda*) formed a complex, multi-faceted centennial offering that provided trenchant commentary on the century-old country, mixing indictment and praise, offsetting despair at failures with hope for the future, and juxtaposing prose and poetry

Whitman's centennial publications were more successful financially than his previous work, in part because of a transatlantic debate that increased his visibility dramatically. He helped spark the controversy when he wrote "Walt Whitman's Actual American Position," a third-person contribution to the *West Jersey Press* in 1876, which offered an exaggerated account of his neglect and argued that he was systematically excluded from American magazines, while leading poets snubbed him when compiling anthologies of poetry. He sent this article to William Michael Rossetti in England, the editor and translator Rudolph Schmidt in Denmark, and the critic and scholar Edward Dowden in Ireland, among others. The debate heated up when Robert Buchanan (famous for his essay on the pre-Raphaelites entitled "The Fleshly School of Poetry") entered the fray, sharply criticizing the treatment of Whitman on the American side of the Atlantic. Bayard Taylor led the opposing camp, defending the American literati's treatment of Whitman. The editor of the popular literary journal *Appleton's* commented astutely that the whole thing smacked of an "advertising trick" by Whitman and his allies to market his works. In fact, this debate did have the practical benefit of increasing sales (Whitman said that English subscribers to the 1876 *Leaves* and *Two Rivulets* "pluck'd me like a brand from the burning, and gave me life again").

The English support of Whitman marked a culmination of interest that had been building since Rossetti's publication of *Poems by Walt Whitman*. Of the many British readers drawn to Whitman through this book, Anne Burrows Gilchrist was among the most important. Married for ten years to the biographer Alexander Gilchrist, until his death in 1861, Anne Gilchrist raised their four children alone and completed her husband's *Life of William Blake*. Mrs Gilchrist wrote a series of letters to Rossetti, which eventually contributed to her insightful essay, "A Woman's Estimate of Walt Whitman" (1870). Mrs Gilchrist and Whitman corresponded for six years, with ardor on her side and caution on his. Then, surprisingly, the poet sent her a ring. His gift was not casual, but neither did it signify in a conventional way. He employed a time-honored symbol *and* strove to make new meaning with it, in this case signaling not romantic love but the loving friendship he was ready to share with Mrs Gilchrist. Eventually, she crossed the Atlantic convinced that she was destined to bear the children of the "tenderest lover." After her arrival in Philadelphia in September 1876, to their mutual credit, they overcame initial awkwardness and developed a warm friendship. She remained in the US for 18 months, during which time Whitman visited almost daily and sometimes lived at the Gilchrist house, where he became part of the family and developed close ties to Anne's children, particularly her son Herbert, a painter. Herbert sketched and painted several portraits of Whitman, including one of him sitting naked by Timber Creek in New Jersey, where he often retreated to recover from the effects of his stroke.

Timber Creek, about twelve miles from Camden, became a kind of sanctuary for Whitman in the years following the centennial celebration. It is the place where he continued to maintain key emotional ties with working-class men, often substantially younger men. His relationship with Doyle had gradually dwindled as the two men saw less and less of one another. At Timber Creek, however, Whitman developed an intimate relationship with a young farmhand named Edward Cattell, who had been introduced to Whitman by Harry Stafford. Herbert Gilchrist visited Timber Creek, too, and Whitman was close to a number of young men who gathered there, but it was Stafford who now displaced Doyle as his special boy friend, his "darling son." Stafford, an emotionally unstable young man of 18 when Whitman first met him in 1876, did odd jobs at the Camden *New*

Republic. The Stafford family regarded Whitman as a type of mentor and were pleased with the poet's interest in the young man. Stafford's mother was especially solicitous of Whitman as he strove to nurse himself back to health after his stroke, through the restorative powers of the natural scene at the Stafford family farm near Timber Creek. The nature of Whitman's relationship with Stafford remains mysterious. We know that the poet and Harry enjoyed wrestling together (leaving John Burroughs dismayed at the way they "cut up like two boys" [Barrus 1931, 164]); that a friendship ring given by Whitman to Stafford went back and forth numerous times (with anguished rhetoric) as the relationship developed; that they shared a room together when traveling; and that they had a photograph taken together in a kind of wedding pose. Whitman and Stafford also discussed attractive women (as the poet had done with Peter Doyle). After Stafford married in 1884, the two men maintained a friendly relationship.

We can get a glimpse of Whitman's complex relationship with Stafford by examining a letter he wrote to Harry (Whitman called him "Hank") on a cold January day in 1881, when Whitman was 62 years old. Twenty-two-year-old Harry – for whom he had served as an intimate mentor – had just been reading a book by Robert Green Ingersoll, the notorious atheist, and had made the mistake of talking with his minister about it. He was now clearly upset both by Ingersoll's arguments about the deleterious effects of religion and by his minister's anger that poor Harry was risking his soul by even reading such trash. Confused and flustered, he wrote to Walt – who had given him Ingersoll's book to read – and sought his advice. Whitman's response to him reveals a great deal about the depth of their relationship and the way that Whitman saw that relationship as interwoven with his deepest beliefs:

Dear Hank –

Dear boy – your letter rec'd & read – Take it easy about the minister & the Ingersoll business – the best answer you can make is to be quiet & good natured & even attentive & *not get mad worth a cent* – True religion (*the most beautiful thing in the whole world,* & the best part of any man's or woman's, or boy's character) consists in *what one does* square and kind & generous & honorable all days, *all the time* – & especially with his own folks & associates & with the poor & illiterate & in devout meditation, & silent thoughts of God, & death – & not at all in what he *says*, nor in Sunday or prayer meeting *gas* – My own opinion is that Ingersoll *talks* too much on his side – a *good life, steady trying to do fair,* & a sweet, tolerant liberal disposition, shines like the sun, tastes like the fresh air of a May morning, blooms like a perfect little flower by the road-side – & all the blowing, talking & powowing *both sides* amounts to little or nothing – Glad, dear boy, you had a good little visit, you & Mont, with me – I enjoyed it too – I am writing this up in the room – the sun shines, but sharp cold & the wind whistling –

Your Walt (*Corr.,* 3:207–8)

Here Whitman gives us his definition of the "good life": "*steady trying to do fair.*" And to achieve that steadiness and fairness, one must cultivate "a sweet, tolerant liberal disposition." It *does* take cultivation, in Whitman's mind, and, with the right kind of nurturing, the result will be "a perfect little flower by the road-side," a strong little flower that can stand up to "all the blowing, talking & powowing *both sides.*" And Whitman, sitting in his little room in Camden with the "sharp cold & the wind whistling" all about him, models this disposition for Harry by emphasizing how, even on this January day, even with a half-paralyzed body, "the sun shines" through all the bluster, how a "tolerant liberal disposition" always "shines like the sun" through "the blowing" that goes on all around it, the "talking and powowing" that is always trying to whip people into taking up sides, narrow their tolerance, whittle their liberal disposition into partisan fervor. That constricting, illiberal zeal is fueled by "Sunday or prayer meeting *gas.*"

Whitman here is casting in terms that Harry can understand precisely what he had said twenty-five years earlier in "Song of Myself," when he had announced that he was through with the "talkers" and "trippers" and "askers" and "contenders":

I have heard what the talkers were talking . . . . the talk of the beginning
    and the end,
But I do not talk of the beginning or the end.
. . .
Trippers and askers surround me,
. . .
Apart from the pulling and hauling stands what I am,
Stands amused, complacent, compassionating, idle, unitary,

Looks down, is erect, bends an arm on an impalpable certain rest,
Looking with sidecurved head curious what will come next,
Both in and out of the game, and watching and wondering at it.

Backward I see in my own days where I sweated through fog with
    linguists and contenders,
I have no mockings or arguments .... I witness and wait. (*LG 1855*,
    14–15)

However much he was the poet of the Open Road, Whitman was
also always the poet "by the road-side," like the little liberal flower he
urged Harry to become, witnessing and waiting, apart from the arguments and the pulling and the hauling, reaching above the fog of the
contenders, into the liberal sunlight, the sunlight that was for Whitman
the emblem of what we might call democratic virtue. As he wrote in
his 1860 poem "To a Common Prostitute," "Not till the sun excludes
you do I exclude you" (*LG*, 387). The good life, he tells young Harry,
"shines like the sun" and brings us "the fresh air of a May morning"
even in the heart of winter. And Whitman teaches Harry that a sunny
disposition will be achieved only if he can "be quiet & good natured &
even attentive & *not get mad worth a cent*." Witness and wait, he advises
Harry; stand apart (by the roadside); stand amused and compassionating
(not impassioned and gassed up).

In this letter to Harry, Whitman's use of the little phrase "by the
road-side" is suggestive, since, when he wrote this note, he had just
been working on rearranging the poems of *Leaves of Grass* for one final
time, and he had created a new cluster of poems, made up of pieces
that spanned his career; he gave this cluster the title "By the Road-
side." His use of the phrase in the context of defining the "good life"
suggests that we might read the odd miscellany of poems he gathered
under that title as a kind of gloss on his conception of what the good
life entailed. Those poems record moments of alert observation of the
world and of his life passing by. They are often brief epiphanies, like
"A Child's Amaze":

Silent and amazed even when a little boy,
I remember I heard the preacher every Sunday put God in his
    statements,
As contending against some being or influence. (*LG*, 275)

Walt, too, like Harry Stafford, had spent some time in church as a young man, and he quickly decided that the preachers seemed more interested in making God a "contender" rather than a "tolerant liberal" force. Amazed at this, Whitman never attended church as an adult, and it would finally be the great atheist Robert Green Ingersoll, the same one who upset Harry, who would speak at Whitman's funeral instead of a minister. In his eulogy, Ingersoll celebrated this quality of virtuous democracy in Whitman: "He was, above all I have known, the poet of humanity, of sympathy . . . He sympathized with the imprisoned and despised, and even on the brow of crime he was great enough to place the kiss of human sympathy" (Ingersoll 1920, 473–4). In his long address, Ingersoll quoted only one line of Whitman's poetry: "One of the greatest lines in our literature is his, and the line is great enough to do honor to the greatest genius that has ever lived. He said, speaking of an outcast: 'Not till the sun excludes you do I exclude you'" (Ingersoll 1920, 474). For Ingersoll, God and religion throughout history had divided, judged, excluded, condemned, separated. Whitman was the opposite force, inclusive as the sun, recognizing and loving all that he encountered. Whitman, in defining what the democratic poet would have to become, put it this way: "He judges not as the judge judges but as the sun falling around a helpless thing." He does not separate the guilty from the innocent, the evil from the good; he simply cares for all. One little poem in "By the Roadside" is just called "Thought":

> Of Justice – as if Justice could be any thing but the same ample law,
>   expounded by natural judges and saviors,
> As if it might be this thing or that thing, according to decisions.
>   (*LG*, 276)

The "ample law" is what the "natural judge," the sun, applies to all things, and it stands above "decisions," which are by definition discriminatory judgments that divide and label and reduce. Another "Thought" in "By the Roadside" is "Of Equality – As if it harmed me, giving others the same chances and rights as myself – As if it were not indispensable to my own rights that others possess the same" (*LG*, 611).

Whitman's good life shines like the sun, then, reaching out to everything in an inclusive embrace that seeks not to exclude but to include. The good life, for him, was finding that all life was good. If we widen our acceptance, stop discriminating, we will find ourselves more at home in a cluttered world. No wonder he celebrated the new technology of photography as the perfect tool of democratic art: while others complained that photography was a flawed representational art because it was indiscriminate and included everything that appeared in a visual field, producing a clutter, Whitman embraced it for exactly that quality: beauty would no longer be defined as that which was selected out and placed above, but rather as that which included all. He once said the real power of photography was that "it lets nature have its way" (*WWC*, 4:125). Fullness of diversity became democratic beauty, and the photograph, with its sensitive plate that absorbed the impression of every detail that formed a scene, became the model for Whitman's absorptive lines, his flowing catalogs that sought to accumulate details toward a diverse unity, excluding nothing, gathering up a grand democratic clutter. "In these *Leaves*," he wrote, "everything is literally photographed" (*NUPM*, 4:1523). An early term for photography was "sun-painting": the sun as a painter did not discriminate and select but instead only accumulated, made room for everything it illuminated. Whitman is our sun-poet, and the good life for him begins with an understanding of the "tolerant liberal disposition" of the sun. Be as still, as patient, as absorptive, as a prepared and waiting photographic plate, welcoming the impress of the infinitely varied world.

But there's also an active component to the good life for Whitman, as he underscores in his advice to Harry: "True religion (*the most beautiful thing in the whole world*, & the best part of any man's or woman's, or boy's character) consists in *what one does* square and kind & generous & honorable all days, *all the time* – & especially with his own folks & associates & with the poor & illiterate & in devout meditation, & silent thoughts of God, & death – & not at all in what he *says*." It is this way of being – of *doing* – in the world that Whitman articulated early on, way back in his preface to his first edition of *Leaves of Grass*, where he instructs us on what we must *do* to live the good life:

> This is what you shall do: Love the earth and sun and the animals, despise riches, give alms to every one that asks, stand up for the stupid and crazy, devote your income and labor to others, hate tyrants, argue not concerning God, have patience and indulgence toward the people,

take off your hat to nothing known or unknown or to any man or number of men, go freely with powerful uneducated persons and with the young and with the mothers of families, read these leaves in the open air every season of every year of your life, re examine all you have been told at school or church or in any book, dismiss whatever insults your own soul, and your very flesh shall be a great poem and have the richest fluency not only in its words but in the silent lines of its lips and face and between the lashes of your eyes and in every motion and joint of your body. (*LG 1855*, v–vi)

Whitman's conception of the good life here is derived from Aristotle, who reasoned that it was a life acted in accord with virtue. Our job is to create a virtuous soul, Aristotle said; the result will be a good life. *Eudaimonia*, the state of contentment brought on by feeling healthy and prosperous and happy, was the "good life" sought by many Greek philosophers, but for Aristotle prosperity and health were often the results of luck or chance, and a happiness based on them was finally empty; true happiness emerged only through virtuous acts. His *Ethics* is a long exploration of what constitutes the "virtuous."

Whitman was a notorious dabbler in philosophy, picking up and jotting down bits and pieces of Greek, French, and German philo-sophical writings throughout his lifetime. In the 1850s, around the time he was writing his preface to *Leaves of Grass*, he was reading Rousseau's *Social Contract*, with the help of a friend who was translat-ing it, and Whitman recorded this summary:

Aristotle had said . . . that men are not equal by nature, but that some were born for slavery, and some for dominion. – Aristotle was right, but he mistook the effect for the cause. Every man that is born in slavery is born for slavery; nothing is more certain. – Slaves lose every-thing in their fetters; even to the desire of quitting them; they love their servitude, as the companions of Ulysses loved their brutishness. If there are slaves by nature, it is because there have been slaves against nature. – Force made the first slavery; cowardice has perpetuated it. (*NUPM*, 5:1848)

Here was the source of Whitman's admonition about what we must *do*: hate tyrants, take hats off to no one, challenge authority as a habit of mind, re-examine everything we've ever been taught. Avoid the fetters, because once they're on, you may have no choice but to love your servitude. His own hatred of American slavery is indicated here, but for him "slavery" was always more than the South's peculiar institution; we were all slaves to habits and conventions and modes of thought that killed a good life just as effectively as chattel slavery.

Another little note Whitman once scribbled about Aristotle is equally revealing: "Aristotle mediums between extremes, also experimental philosophy. (It seems to be the substratum on which are based modern literature, education, and very largely modern character)" (*NUPM*, 5:1884). This little note indicates Whitman's awareness of Aristotle's belief that virtue comes in finding the middle way. Temperance, generosity, prudence, magnanimity: all these "middle" virtues (mediating the extremes, as generosity, for example, mediates between profligacy and parsimony) Whitman could find in phrenology as easily as in Aristotle, but, wherever he found it, he took the lesson to heart, and it is everywhere in his writings, as in the 1855 preface: "The soul has that measureless pride which consists in never acknowledging any lessons but its own. But it has sympathy as measureless as its pride and the one balances the other and neither can stretch too far while it stretches in company with the other. The inmost secrets of art sleep with the twain" (*LG 1855*, vi). To find that middle ground between pride and sympathy was, for Whitman, the great challenge of living in a democracy – to find a way of celebrating individualism while also celebrating the unity of the diverse collective. He announced this middle ground in the poem that in 1870 he placed first in *Leaves of Grass*:

> One's-Self I sing, a simple separate person,
> Yet utter the word Democratic, the word En-Masse. (*LG*, 1)

Or, as he once told another young Camden friend, Horace Traubel: "Be individualistic, be individualistic, be not too damned individualistic." Always seeking the moderate response is what stands behind Whitman's warning to Harry Stafford to "*not get mad worth a cent*," to live the "*good life, steady trying to do fair*." Steadiness, a temperate temper, standing apart: it's all part of Whitman's recipe for the good life.

Whitman embraced one other key aspect of Aristotle's examination of the good life, and that was friendship: "For without friends," Aristotle said, "no one would choose to live, though he had all other goods." Aristotle offers a kind of anatomy of friendship in his *Ethics*, privileging what he defines as virtuous friendship, a "friendship for the good," that emerges when two people act together to develop the overall goodness of each other. Like Aristotle, Whitman believed this kind of relationship was best experienced by an older male with a younger male. Through his lifetime, Whitman had his photograph taken often, but almost always alone; there are no photos of him with any family member or with his adult friends, but there is a series of photos of him with his young boy friends, and they record a kind of restless seeking of this aspect of the good life. In the 1860s, he was photographed with Peter Doyle; in the 1870s with Harry Stafford; in the 1880s with Bill Duckett; and in the 1890s with Warren Fritzinger (see chapter 7 on Duckett and Fritzinger). Whitman never published any of these odd, wedding-like portraits, but he kept them near him at all times. He sought some radical and unnamed new affectional structure for which he had only old and inappropriate terms of relationship.

The good life for Walt Whitman was finally, then, a lonely (but not unhappy) affair. Growing up in a largely dysfunctional family, finding his affectional energies directed toward males, he knew from early on that for him the good life would not be the conventional arrangement of a wife and family and stable home. He built a poetry that was based on the idea of an "I" that was always fluid and changing, on the move, loath to settle down, cruising. His expansive, democratic persona would wither and die if it ever began to focus its attention on a single person or place. He invented a poetic syntax of continual forgetting and moving. What sustained him throughout his life was his series of relationships with young men, right up to the end when his so-called disciples nursed him and held him and kissed him, just as he had done with all those hundreds of injured and dying boy-soldiers in the Civil War.

So it is fitting that a group of English men – an array of writers, intellectuals, shopkeepers, and laborers – also regarded Whitman as a figure of pivotal importance. These men were struggling to establish a positive identity based on same-sex love (what was just then beginning to be called "homosexuality") within a culture which increasingly categorized such love as morbid and criminal. Edward Carpenter, a major interpreter of Whitman in England, first came to Camden to visit Whitman in 1877 and returned again in 1884. Carpenter influenced various artists, intellectuals, and sex radicals through the example of his life (notable for his decades-long relationship with a working-class man, George Merrill), and through his writings, including his

Whitman-inspired poetry in *Towards Democracy* (1883–1902), his many essays, and later his *Days with Walt Whitman* (1906), a memoir of his association with Whitman and an analysis of Whitman's work and influence. Carpenter helped spread word of Whitman to the labor movement in England, where the poet's language of comradeship was employed by English followers eager to advance a more egalitarian society. Many other people made pilgrimages to Camden in these years, with Oscar Wilde among the most famous. In 1882 Wilde drank elderberry wine with the poet, enthused over his Greek qualities, and declared that there is "no one in this great wide world of America whom I love and honor so much."

CHAPTER 7

Dying into *Leaves*

Whitman's work, repeatedly endorsed by English readers and by European admirers, especially in France and Germany, received a further boost in 1881 when a mainstream Boston publisher, James R. Osgood & Co., decided to issue *Leaves of Grass* under its imprint. Osgood, though struggling financially, had a reputable publishing house, with a list that once included Emerson, Nathaniel Hawthorne, Mark Twain, and Charles Dickens. Just as Thayer and Eldridge had offered Whitman respectable Boston publication over twenty years earlier, so he could once again look forward to wide distribution, high visibility, and institutional validation (a paradoxical idea, of course, for a renegade poet). He again traveled to Boston to oversee the printing of his book, and he spent his time there in the Rand, Avery, & Co. typesetting shop, where he had worked on the 1860 edition. "I am coming on to see to & oversee it, every page – will take six or eight weeks," he wrote (*Corr.*, 3:236). Once again, however, he encountered problems. The Boston district attorney, Oliver Stevens, wrote to Osgood on March 1, 1882: "We are of the opinion that this book is such a book as brings it within the provisions of the Public Statutes respecting obscene literature and suggest the propriety of withdrawing the same from circulation and suppressing the editions thereof" (*Corr.*, 3:267n). The notorious moralist Anthony Comstock and the New England Society for the Suppression of Vice encouraged this proceeding, but numerous reviews had also predicted trouble for the book.

Osgood lacked financial resources (and perhaps the will) to fight Stevens and so sought a compromise, hoping that the poet would agree to excise objectionable passages; Whitman, thinking that the required alterations might involve only ten lines "& half a dozen words or phrases," looked for a way around the ban. But once he recognized how thoroughgoing the changes would need to be, his position stiffened. The offending passages appeared in "Song of Myself," "From Pent-up Aching Rivers," "A Woman Waits for Me," "I Sing the Body Electric," "Spontaneous Me," "The Dalliance of the Eagles," "Native Moments," "By Blue Ontario's Shore," "To a Common Prostitute," "Unfolded Out of the Folds," "The Sleepers," and "Faces." For most poems, only particular passages or words were at issue, but the district attorney insisted that "A Woman Waits for Me" and "To a Common Prostitute" had to be removed entirely. Intriguingly, the "Calamus" section and other poems treating male–male love raised no concern, perhaps because the male–male poems infrequently venture beyond handholding and hugging while the male–female poems are frank about copulation. Whitman wrote to Osgood: "The list whole & several is rejected by me, & will not be thought of under any circumstances" (*Corr.*, 3:270). Osgood stopped selling *Leaves of Grass* and transferred the plates to Whitman, who took them to Rees Welsh, a Philadelphia publisher. Rees Welsh printed around 6,000 copies of the book, and initial sales were brisk. David McKay of Rees Welsh was particularly supportive of Whitman; soon McKay broke away and began publishing Whitman through his own firm. Another benefit of the suppression controversy was that it helped restore an important friendship with O'Connor, who ignored past differences and came to Whitman's defense with a vigorous essay, "Mr. Comstock as Cato the Censor," in the New York *Tribune*. O'Connor heaped praise on Whitman, argued that *Leaves of Grass* (like the *Decameron*) was a "book [that] belonged to literature and not to lust," and invoked Emerson's praise as further evidence of its high-mindedness (Loving 1978, 234).

Whitman's "Memorandum at a Venture," an essay written in the same year *Leaves* was banned in Boston, argues that the "current prurient, conventional treatment of sex is the main formidable obstacle" to women's advancement in business, politics, and social life (*PW*, 2:494). His depictions of women have been criticized (for example, D. H. Lawrence claimed that Whitman reduced women to wombs). While *Leaves of Grass* clearly emphasized motherhood, Whitman also valued other roles for women. In fact, the women he most celebrated – among them the critic and reformer Margaret Fuller, the radical reform writer Frances Wright, the novelist George Sand, and the eccentric critic Delia Bacon – were those who challenged conventional social arrangements. Some nineteenth-century women criticized Whitman: the suffragist Elizabeth Cady Stanton, for example, thought he presented a skewed portrayal of women's sexuality in "A Woman Waits for Me," even though she endorsed the freedom and assertiveness Whitman insisted on when he said, in the same poem, that women must "know how to swim, row, ride, wrestle, shoot, run, strike, retreat, advance, resist, defend themselves" (*LG*, 102). Most women of his day looked beyond his occasional lapses, and several wrote him letters praising the liberating value of his poetry. In addition, notable writers ranging from Kate Chopin to Charlotte Perkins Gilman to Edith Wharton invoked his work in their own writings both because of what he said about women and because of his vision of comradeship. They perceived that Whitman's comradeship – with its promise of mutuality and equality – could be retooled to critique hierarchical relations between men and women.

The autobiographical prose work *Specimen Days,* issued as a counterpart to the 1881–2 *Leaves of Grass,* was described by Whitman as the "most wayward, spontaneous, fragmentary book ever printed" (*PW*, 1:1). The spontaneity could be questioned, since it was a multiply re-scripted work: the powerful sections on the war were first drafted at hospital bedsides, often reworked for initial publication in newspapers, further refined for use in *Memoranda During the War,* and reshaped once again for publication in the war section of *Specimen Days.* The book is an unusual autobiography in many ways, including its emphasis on the middle and late stages of life rather than the early ones. Whitman reveals little about a central mystery: the development of the first edition of *Leaves of Grass.* After a concise treatment of his family background, he moves quickly past his "long foreground" to focus on the Civil War. Knowing that his direct and extensive connection to the war set him apart from other writers, he argues that the hospitals were central to the war just as the war was a defining experience for America. He famously said "my book and the war are one," asserting implicitly that his life and the war are one (*LG*, 5). It is the love, sacrifice, comradeship, and courage of the hospitals that Whitman now decides to record as central to his life, not the creating of *Leaves of Grass,* a book of world-wide significance. He attributes his paralysis to the war, and now, after the conflict, the crisis of his culture remains inscribed on his body. His personal efforts to overcome paralysis are mirrored in the larger cultural efforts to find new vitality and hope despite the injuries of the past, the fundamental damage already done.

Following the war section of *Specimen Days*, Whitman shifts to nature reflections evoked by the Stafford farm setting at Timber Creek, where he underwent a self-imposed, idiosyncratic, but effective regimen of physical therapy (including wrestling with saplings and taking mud baths) to restore his body from the ravages of stroke. He also describes his 1879 trip to participate in the quarter-centennial celebration of the Kansas settlement and to visit his brother Jeff in St Louis. Whitman traveled as far as Denver and the Rockies, finding in the landscape a grandeur that matched his earlier visions of it and a ruggedness that he believed justified his approach to American poetry. Throughout *Specimen Days*, he keeps in mind his standing in the national pantheon. In "My Tribute to Four Poets" and in discussions of Emerson, Henry Wadsworth Longfellow, Edgar Allan Poe, and Carlyle, Whitman seeks to position himself as magnanimous in relation to his key predecessors. Showing a new generosity, he now praises fellow poets he once belittled for their "perpetual, pistareen, paste-pot work" (*PW*, 2:388–9). Putting aside earlier slights, he takes a large-minded position: he shows no ill will toward Emerson, Whittier, or Bryant, all of whom, in the 1870s, had compiled anthologies of poetry that pointedly excluded Whitman's work altogether.

Specimen Days, long neglected in criticism, is now being read by many critics as an eccentric and experimental work, a fitting counterpart in prose to Whitman's radically new poetry. One useful way of thinking of the book, as George Hutchinson has noted, is in terms of "life review," the psychological process of coming to terms with death by making sense of personal history, the contour of life (Hutchinson 1987, 4). As the number of elderly Americans increases in the coming years, Whitman's late work may be re-evaluated and even more greatly admired. There is much to be learned from his capacity to remake himself and his project under very trying circumstances, and from his ability to read an individual life in terms of larger historical, cultural, and natural processes.

Whitman found another opportunity to shape his life story when the Canadian Richard Maurice Bucke undertook the first full-length biography of the poet, published as *Walt Whitman* in 1883. The book appeared through David McKay, who was establishing himself as the primary publisher of Whitman and Whitman-related materials. Bucke was immediately enthralled when he first read Whitman in 1867, though his initial overtures toward the poet went nowhere when Whitman did not answer his letters. Once the two men met in the late 1870s, however, they began a key friendship and literary relationship. Bucke was fascinated by science and mysticism: he was superintendent of the largest mental asylum in North America and the author of *Man's Moral Nature* and *Cosmic Consciousness*. He believed that Whitman's achievement put him near the head of a group of luminaries including Moses, Buddha, Jesus, Socrates, and Wordsworth. Whitman provided information for the biography when he visited Bucke in Ontario for four months in the summer of 1880, yet even after Whitman drafted parts of this study and edited much that Bucke wrote, he did not think the book created a truthful portrait. Interestingly, he himself excised some of Bucke's better insights, including his accounts of Whitman's motherly nature and of the intimate friendship the poet struck up with a Canadian soldier while traveling with Bucke.

Whitman's life story was also bound up with Lincoln's, and the poet worked hard to strengthen that connection. For about a decade, beginning in the late 1870s, Whitman regularly offered lectures on Lincoln. These lectures, complementing his famous elegies, "When Lilacs Last in the Dooryard Bloom'd" and "O Captain! My Captain!," brought Whitman much-needed income, while underscoring again his connection with the war and the martyred president. These Lincoln lectures were as close as Whitman ever came to becoming the wandering lecturer he had dreamed of being in his youth. He usually concluded with "O Captain!," signaling his willingness to serve the role of popular elegist despite his personal misgivings about the conventionality of the poem.

In the 1880s, as Whitman was compiling authoritative versions of his writings and overseeing various accounts of his life, he was also putting his domestic arrangements in better order. He had been living with his brother George's family, but when George retired and moved his family to a farm outside of town, Whitman refused to leave Camden. With royalty money from the 1881–2 edition of *Leaves* and a loan from publisher George W. Childs, the poet purchased "a little old shanty of my own" (*Corr.*, 3:368). In March, 1884, he moved into the only home he ever owned. The poet thought that the two-story frame house at 328 Mickle Street, lacking a furnace and in need of repairs, suited him well. His personal room quickly took on a distinctive aura: many visitors noted how the poet resided in a sea of chaotic papers. One guest remarked: "I found Whitman calmly sitting in the midst of such utter and appalling literary confusion, I wondered for a moment how he breathed – vast heaps of everything piled about him. It seemed as though an earthquake had thrown all the life and literature of the hour, everything, in fact, into ruins, but the old god" (quoted in Haven 2004, 13).

With Whitman becoming decreasingly mobile, Thomas Donaldson, a Philadelphia lawyer, devised a plan in 1885 to get the poet a horse and buggy by asking 35 men to donate 10 dollars apiece. Bill Duckett, a teenage boy who boarded briefly with Whitman and his house-keeper Mrs Davis, often accompanied Whitman on his drives. As a carriage driver and companion, Duckett held a role in some ways similar to that of Fred Vaughan, Peter Doyle, and Harry Stafford. Yet it is unlikely that Duckett meant as much to the poet as these earlier intimate companions. Whitman was, however, photographed with the youth, once while Duckett was driving Whitman's horse and carriage, and another time in one of those noteworthy pictures (similar to wedding poses) in which Whitman appears with various younger men – Doyle, Stafford, and Duckett himself – creating an iconography for relationships based on "calamus" friendship. The friendship with Duckett eventually ended. Mrs Davis took him to court for failing to pay his boarding bill, though the young man claimed he owed nothing since the poet had invited him into his house.

Other efforts to aid the poet were less successful. When several individuals – William Sloane Kennedy, a member of Whitman's inner circle, Sylvester Baxter, a Boston journalist, and Henry B. Lovering, a congressman from Massachusetts – attempted to secure a war pension for Whitman, the poet himself refused to support this effort. He wrote to Baxter that he did "not consent to being an applicant for a pension as spoken of – I do not deserve it" (*Corr.*, 4:56). Nonetheless, the mere rumor that Whitman was being considered for a pension was enough to provoke Thomas Wentworth Higginson to vigorously oppose the idea in the pages of *Harper's Bazaar*. Higginson ridiculed Whitman's manhood:

Figure 6 Photograph by Dr William Reeder of Whitman in his Camden, New Jersey, home (1891). Ed Folsom collection.

There is, it is true, a class of men whose claims are intermediate between those of the soldiers and those of the women. There were many men who, being rejected from enlistment for physical defects, sought honorably to serve their country as hospital nurses or agents of the Sanitary Commission. A beginning has been made in the way of pensioning these men in the case of the proposed pension for Mr. Whitman, the poet; although he . . . deliberately preferred service in the hospital rather than in the field. (Higginson 1887, 162)

Higginson (who had met the poet back in 1860 in Boston when Higginson was actively supporting the radical abolitionist John Brown) had taken a powerful disliking to Whitman, and in a series of essays (including, ultimately, an obituary notice) he attacked Whitman on various grounds including the poet's fondness for men. Higginson's animosity led some in Whitman's circle to conclude that he was behind the banning of *Leaves* in Boston, though no evidence has been found to support that suspicion.

Lacking a guaranteed source of income, Whitman helped himself by peppering periodicals in these years with poems and essays that kept his name before the public and brought in needed money. He published more than eighty poems in periodicals in the last decade of his life. (This was more than half of all the poems he published in periodicals from 1855 to 1892.) The poems written after 1881 did not alter the fundamental shape of his life's work. In fact, he made a point of leaving the basic structure of *Leaves* unchanged following the suppression controversy. The late poems – typically appearing first in a periodical and then in a separate volume such as *November Boughs* or *Good-Bye My Fancy* – were placed in appendices or, as he called them, "annexes" when he finally incorporated them into *Leaves of Grass*, the main book.

November Boughs (1888) was a volume containing 64 poems, collected under the title "Sands at Seventy," and various prose works previously published in periodicals. Some of the prose writings are effective and accomplished pieces, especially "Father Taylor (and Oratory)," "Robert Burns as Poet and Person," and "Slang in America." *Good-Bye My Fancy* (1891) was published initially as a miscellany of prose and verse. Whitman later printed 31 poems from the book in "Good-Bye my Fancy: 2d Annex" to *Leaves of Grass* (1891–2). While he lacked the poetic daring, range, and acuity of his early years, he still could write engaging poems such as "A Twilight Song," "Osceola," and "To the Sun-Set Breeze." "A Twilight Song" is a haunted poem, capturing Whitman's final attempt to bring the forgotten Civil War dead ("each name recall'd by me from out the darkness and death's ashes") to the attention of a nation that had, by the end of the poet's life, turned away from memories of the war. "Osceola" recalls the death of the Seminole leader Osceola in the 1830s (he "literally died of 'a broken heart,'" Whitman writes), a death that seems to presage the loss of American Indian culture as well as to evoke Whitman's own impending death. "To the Sun-Set Breeze" is a delicate poem capturing a moment when the aged and sick poet is refreshed by a gentle wind that brings to his fading senses a touch of "the sky, the prairies vast" and eventually "the globe itself swift-swimming in space"; the twentieth-century poet Ezra Pound, usually a Whitman detractor, would praise the "deliberate artistry" of this poem (quoted in Perlman et al. 1998, 113).

Whitman continued writing, "garrulous" to the very end, and this resulted in a brave and often painful poetry recording invalidism and old age. He worried that his new writing might undermine his previous accomplishments:

As I sit writing here, sick and grown old,
Not my least burden is that dulness of the years, querilities,
Ungracious glooms, aches, lethargy, constipation, whimpering *ennui*,
May filter in my daily songs. (*LG*, 509–10)

Aware that illness had overtaken him, that the national fame he sought was spotty, and that his celebration of the human body and his own body in particular could now be seen as a cruel joke, Whitman nonetheless mustered the honesty and drive to record his life – with its diminishment and indignities – candidly and courageously.

A crucial development of Whitman's final years was the growth of his friendship with Horace Traubel, who was nearly forty years younger than the poet. Traubel met Whitman when the poet first moved to Camden, but starting in the late 1880s he became a daily visitor and recorder of Whitman's conversation. Later he would become one of the three executors of the estate and a vigorous defender of the poet's reputation. Traubel was devoted to the poet and believed that all that Whitman said was memorable: he kept detailed notes of his daily exchanges with the poet and published three large volumes of them as *With Walt Whitman in Camden* (six more volumes, based on Traubel's manuscripts, were published after his death). *With Walt Whitman in Camden* is the longest biography yet written of an American. Fittingly, it is an extraordinary, experimental work, full of riches that have yet to be appreciated because of the long delay of its full publication in print and because of its sheer unwieldiness (it is nearly 5,000 pages long). Because one of his parents was a Jew, the other a Christian, Traubel felt especially suited to interpret Whitman, the poet of inclusiveness. Traubel, who was forced to resign from his job in a bank because of his socialist views, urged Whitman to express support for socialism. After Whitman's death, Traubel became editor of the *Conservator*, a journal dedicated to continuing the poet's message. Traubel was the pivotal figure among Whitman's American disciples, a group sometimes disparagingly called the "hot little prophets." Although Traubel – married and with a child – had at least one passionate love affair with a man, he was characteristic of Whitman's American followers in trying to protect Whitman's reputation by resisting attempts to associate the poet with homosexuality, even going so far as to refer to same-sex love as "muck and rot" (Krieg 1996–7, 91).

The American disciples had counterparts in England. J. W. Wallace was the indefatigable leader of a group of socialists (sometimes known as "Bolton College") there, in Lancashire, who ardently admired Whitman. Wallace visited Camden in the autumn of 1891 to see the "prophet" of a new socialist religion. Wallace's group was confident of its place in history: "*We* stand in closest relation to Walt Whitman – the divinely inspired prophet of world democracy" (Salveson 1996–7, 65). Other active members of the group were Fred Wild, a cotton waste merchant, and Dr John Johnston, a general practitioner, who corresponded with the poet, photographed him, and, with Wallace, wrote about him in *Visits to Walt Whitman in 1890–1891 by Two Lancashire Friends*.

Whitman looked for his most enthusiastic audience to come from the US, though he welcomed the unexpected support he received from English readers. Still, at times he found some of his supporters trying. John Addington Symonds, the poet, student of sexuality, and classical scholar, began in the 1870s to question Whitman about the meaning of the "Calamus" cluster. Did it authorize sexual relations between men? Interested in the same-sex attachments depicted in *Leaves of Grass*, Symonds did not want to explicate the poems without reassurance from Whitman, something the poet refused to give. (Symonds's hesitancy resulted from his earlier disastrous "outing" – to use an anachronistic term – of Dr Charles Vaughan, headmaster of Harrow, who had an affair with a student, Symonds's friend Alfred

Pretor.) Whitman was eventually so annoyed by Symonds's questioning that in 1890 the poet concocted a lie of grand proportions: "Tho' always unmarried I have had six children – two are dead – One living southern grandchild, fine boy, who writes to me occasionally. Circumstances connected with their benefit and fortune have separated me from intimate relations" (*Corr.*, 5:73). The outrageousness of Whitman's claim – the flamboyance of his story – signaled something different and more complex than a simple denial. He evaded Traubel's inquiries, too, repeatedly suggesting that he had a great secret to divulge, but refusing to tell it. Whitman wanted to cultivate sexual mystery rather than clarity, and he was not going to reduce his life or thought to narrow and distorting labels or answers, especially on anyone else's terms.

Leaves of Grass took its final shape as authorized by the poet in the "deathbed" edition, technically a reissue of the 1881–2 edition with supplemental material, which appeared in Whitman's final year of life. The first printing was a paperback copy to make sure it reached the poet before his death. He concluded the book with an expanded version of "A Backward Glance O'er Travel'd Roads," an essay that had appeared earlier, in parts, in the *Critic* and in the *New York Star*. "A Backward Glance" and the 1855 preface are the two essays that frame *Leaves of Grass*, beginning his first book of poetry and closing his final one. If the preface is brash, irreverent, and forward looking, "A Backward Glance" is dignified, conciliatory, and retrospective. He explains, in the latter essay, his purpose:

> to articulate and faithfully express in literary or poetic form, and uncompromisingly, my own physical, emotional, moral, intellectual, and æsthetic Personality, in the midst of, and tallying, the momentous spirit and facts of its immediate days, and of current America – and to exploit that Personality, identified with place and date, in a far more candid and comprehensive sense than any hitherto poem or book. (*LG*, 563)

Leaves of Grass was autobiographical but not an autobiography – as much a record of a culture as of a person.

In his final months, Whitman was very sick, beset by an array of ailments, and he seemed to endure through sheer force of will. For some time, he had been preparing for his death. He had a large mausoleum built in Camden's Harleigh Cemetery, on a plot given to him in 1885, shortly after the cemetery was opened. The tomb was paid for in part by Whitman with money donated to him for buying a house in the country and in part by one of his literary executors, Thomas Harned. (Eventually, several family members – George, Hannah, Louisa, Edward, and his parents – were reinterred in the same tomb, on which the inscription reads simply "Walt Whitman.") On December 24, 1891, the poet composed his last will and testament. In an earlier will of 1873 he had bequeathed his silver watch to Peter Doyle, but now, with Doyle largely absent from his life, he made changes, giving his gold watch to Traubel and a silver one to Harry Stafford.

Frederick Warren Fritzinger ("Warry"), a former sailor, nursed Whitman in his final illness. Whitman liked Warry's touch, a blend of masculine strength and feminine tenderness. The poet's last words – a request to be moved in bed, "Shift, Warry" – were addressed to Fritzinger. The poet died on March 26, 1892, his hand resting in that of Traubel. The cause of death was miliary tuberculosis, with other contributing factors. The autopsy revealed that one lung had completely collapsed and the other was working only at one-eighth capacity; his heart was surrounded by a number of small abscesses and about two and a half quarts of water. According to Daniel Longaker, Whitman's physician in the final year, the autopsy showed Whitman to be free of alcoholism or syphilis. Longaker rejected the "slanderous accusations that debauchery and excesses of various kinds caused or contributed to his break-down" (Traubel et al. 1893, 410).

In "Poets to Come" Whitman claimed: "I am a man who, sauntering along without fully stopping, turns a casual look upon you and then averts his face, / Leaving it to you to prove and define it, / Expecting the main things from you" (*LG*, 14). That casual look has had an uncanny impact on countless followers who have sought to complete Whitman's project and thereby to better know themselves. The responses have ranged from indictments to accolades. Some poets mimic his cadences or style, but many poets have understood, with William Carlos Williams, that the only way to write like Whitman is to write unlike Whitman, to forge a new kind of poetry instead of to imitate a poetry that already exists. To an unusual degree, however, Whitman's legacy has not been limited to poetry. He has had an extensive and often unpredictable impact on fiction, film, architecture, music, painting, dance, and other arts.

We've noted that Whitman said, "my book and the war are one." He might have said as well that his book and the United States are one. Whitman, a writer who strove to define national identity and to imagine an inclusive society, has been of crucial importance to writers from various racial and ethnic groups who extended, refined, rewrote, battled, endorsed, and sometimes rejected the poet's work. Recent critics sometimes find fault with Whitman for his shortcomings and occasional failure to live up to his own finest ideals. But writers as diverse as Michael Gold, Langston Hughes, Muriel Rukeyser, Allen Ginsberg, June Jordan, Garrett Hongo, Sherman Alexie, Rudulfo Anaya, and Yusef Komunyakaa have, with rare exceptions, appreciated Whitman's sympathy, generosity, and capaciousness. Whitman's bold claim of 1855 that "the proof of a poet is that his country absorbs him as affectionately as he has absorbed it" is justified by his absorption into American culture (*LG*, 729). Over a century after his death, Whitman is a vital presence in American cultural memory. Television shows depict him. Musicians allude to him. Schools and bridges bear his name. His name can also be found on truck stops, apartment complexes, parks, think tanks, summer camps, corporate centers, and shopping malls. And he has enjoyed an international renown that is as remarkable as is his reception in American culture. Perhaps William Faulkner can match Whitman's impact in South America, but no US writer, including Faulkner, has had a comparable influence worldwide. *Leaves of Grass* has been translated in complete editions in Spanish, French, German, Italian, Chinese, and Japanese, and partial translations have appeared in all major languages. Whitman's influence is due to his literary qualities as well as his standing as a political prophet. Not only has he served as a major icon for socialists and communists, but he has also been invoked on occasion by writers and politicians on the far right, including even the National Socialists in Germany. In general, however, Whitman has been most influential in liberal circles as a writer who articulated the beauty, power, and always incompletely fulfilled promise of democracy and camaraderie.

APPENDIX

What Whitman Left Us

We have seen how Whitman re-scripted his own works in manifold ways, but the re-scripting of his writing did not stop at his death. Editors during his own lifetime, including the British writers William Michael Rossetti and Ernest Rhys, remade his work in new ways, expurgating and pruning and rearranging and issuing it in "selected" editions. The rewriting of Whitman intensified in the years following his death, and so no story of re-scripting Whitman would be complete without an account of how his work has been reshaped as a result of the practices of the editorial projects dedicated to collecting all of his writing and making it widely available. These projects have reformulated his work in accordance with their reigning editorial policies and the demands of the media in which they have worked.

The first large-scale attempt to gather everything Whitman wrote was undertaken in the decade after his death and was overseen by his literary executors, Horace Traubel, Richard Maurice Bucke, and Thomas B. Harned. Issued in ten volumes in 1902 by G. P. Putnam's Sons, *The Complete Writings of Walt Whitman* appeared in seven different "editions," from standard to deluxe (the most expensive editions contained an actual Whitman manuscript tipped into the first volume of the set). Fewer than 1,500 copies of the *Complete Writings* were printed, and the volumes quickly became collector's items. In addition to a three-volume "deathbed" edition of *Leaves of Grass*, the *Complete Writings* contained Whitman's major prose publications, including *Specimen Days* and "Democratic Vistas," and a potpourri of other materials – his Civil War letters to his mother, his letters to Peter Doyle, an apparently random gathering of manuscript fragments, and some criticism about

Whitman. Also included was the first attempt at a variorum edition of *Leaves*, beginning to track the thousands of changes Whitman made in the book over its six editions.

The 1902 *Complete Writings* was a luxurious edition that served to memorialize Whitman and packaged his work in a form that clearly indicated (and argued for) his importance as a writer, at a time when his status as one of America's great authors was anything but secure. Anyone looking at this edition of his work knew immediately that it *looked* like the work of a major author – it was a multi-volume set, bound handsomely, printed on fine paper, with scholarly apparatus. But by the mid-twentieth century, scholars realized that the volumes in the *Complete Writings* had long outlived their usefulness and that it was time for a completely new attempt to gather the massive amount of Whitman material, as researchers and archivists cataloged and continued to turn up thousands of his letters, newspaper articles, early stories, notebooks, daybooks, and manuscript fragments. Scholarly practices had evolved as well, and the *Complete Writings* had come to seem dated and out of fashion. By the mid-twentieth century, Whitman's reputation was secure, and a major writer now needed a major new scholarly edition. In 1955, one hundred years after the appearance of the first edition of *Leaves of Grass*, and forty-five years after the *Complete Writings* was published, New York University Press announced a monumental new project, called *The Collected Writings of Walt Whitman*.

A relatively young group of 12 scholars joined forces on this editorial undertaking that would end up consuming a major part of their professional lives. These scholars announced that the new edition would be complete by the early 1960s. This timetable was almost immediately abandoned, however, and the *Collected Writings* became a half-century-long attempt to compile all of Whitman's writings, to be "absolutely 'complete'" (as the editors put it), and to include his various volumes of poetry and prose, along with all his correspondence, notebooks, daybooks, manuscripts, journalism, and uncollected poetry and fiction. Today, a half-century after the announcement of its birth, the Whitman *Collected Writings*, like virtually every other monumental edition begun back in the 1950s, remains incomplete, and even the finished individual volumes have turned out to be not nearly as finished as everyone expected they would be. Previously undiscovered materials continued to surface, rendering the printed volumes outdated almost by the time they appeared.

The *Collected Writings* now consists of 25 volumes (the 22 volumes originally published by New York University Press, 2 additional volumes published by Peter Lang, and another volume published by the University of Iowa Press). New York University Press, as the original publisher, issued six volumes of correspondence, six volumes of notebooks and unpublished prose manuscripts, three volumes of daybooks and notebooks, two volumes of published prose, one volume of early poetry and fiction, a three-volume variorum of the printed poems, and one volume of a "reader's edition" of the poetry. These are impressive accomplishments. Still, after four decades of energetic work by a team of eight scholars, and the support of an additional six scholars on the editorial board, many of the original goals of the New York University Press edition have been left unrealized. Some of the original intentions of the project were altered along the way. Whitman's journalism, which appeared from 1834 right through to his death in 1892, was intended to be a key part of the *Collected Writings*, but, because of delays in preparing the manuscript, the projected six volumes were abandoned by New York University Press altogether. Only in the last few years have the first two volumes appeared, issued by another publisher; it is questionable whether the remaining volumes will ever be published. Edwin Haviland Miller's magisterial five-volume edition of Whitman's correspondence appeared over an eight-year period in the 1960s, and by the time the fifth volume came out, it already contained an "Addenda" of 65 letters discovered during the eight years the earlier volumes had been appearing; they were now forever out of order, out of chronology, stuck at the back of the set, a permanent mar on the collection. Nine years later, New York University Press issued a slim sixth volume of correspondence, this time called a "Supplement," with 100 more letters, and 14 years later the *Walt Whitman Quarterly Review* published a hundred-page "Second Supplement" with nearly fifty more. Miller is now deceased, and Ted Genoways has published a third and fourth supplement of nearly a hundred letters with the *Walt Whitman Quarterly Review*; he recently edited these as a supplemental volume seven of the *Correspondence*, published by the University of Iowa Press. That volume came out in 2004, and after only a couple of months several more letters had already surfaced.

This story could be repeated across the range of the materials the *Collected Writings* set out to collect: poetry, prose essays, autobiography, fiction, notebooks, prose manuscripts, poetry manuscripts, journalism. In all cases, Whitman remains, as he once described himself, "garrulous to the very last"; it is as if he miraculously continues to generate letters and other manuscripts today at the same rate as when he was alive. His writings are such a mass and scatter that any "complete" print edition is doomed to become increasingly incomplete, patched-together, more difficult to use – eventually as chaotic as the materials it sets out to organize. Materials become jumbled out of sequence or are left uncollected. Indices are rendered incomplete or are never created. New York University Press has issued no volumes in the Whitman edition since 1984, and the project has sputtered to a close, occasionally coming back to life in the anomalous though important additional volumes from other presses. Meanwhile, it has become ever more apparent that the *Collected Writings* will always remain woefully incomplete. All members of the editorial board are now deceased.

So, 40 years after the *Collected Writings* was announced, we joined with other scholars in inaugurating a new project called the *Walt Whitman Archive* (www.whitmanarchive.org), dedicated to gathering Whitman's writing, this time in an electronic environment. Like the editors of the *Collected Writings*, we, as editors of the *Archive*, have an ambitious long-term goal: the creation of a vast electronic scholarly resource that will eventually include in one online site the full range of work by and about the poet. If the *Collected Writings* is best described as an *edition*, the *Walt Whitman Archive* is best described as a *digital thematic research collection*, a newly emerging literary form (Palmer 2004).

The *Walt Whitman Archive* functions as an edition and more: it embraces many types of materials not ordinarily part of standard print editions devoted to an individual writer. At present, these include teaching materials, a substantial biography of the poet, all 130 photographs of Whitman (with full annotations), finding guides to manuscripts, a regularly updated annotated bibliography of scholarship since 1975, a growing body of critical work, and a considerable amount of contextual material, both encyclopedia entries about various topics relating to Whitman and selected writings by his associates. Also included is a great deal of material related to the building of the site: essays about the *Archive*, technical documentation, text encoding guidelines for the staff and for curious visitors, and more. The *Whitman Archive* is attempting to scrupulously document its course, false steps and all, because of a conviction that the shift from print to electronic editing is a matter of real consequence. Early experiments in electronic editing may well be of considerable interest to future scholars.

The *Whitman Archive* is addressing the omissions of the *Collected Writings* on both a small and a large scale. That is, we have located many individual items overlooked by our predecessors. At the same time, we are freshly editing whole categories of writing and recorded speech missing from the *Collected Writings*. In some cases what is absent from the *Collected Writings* was meant to be included, but the work was never completed. The three-volume Variorum Edition of *Leaves of Grass*, for example, was originally slated to record all the manuscripts, periodical publications, and book publications of Whitman's poems, but it dealt, finally, only with the book publications, leaving the important manuscript origins and early periodical versions unavailable to scholars and students.

The emphasis in the *Collected Writings* on a single authoritative text shapes that project's presentation of *Leaves of Grass*. The Variorum and the Comprehensive Reader's Edition both use the final "deathbed" edition of *Leaves* as the copy text, and so missing from the 25 volumes is a straightforward printing of the 1855 *Leaves of Grass*, one of the most important documents in American literary history. The heavy investment in Whitman's so-called "deathbed" edition (as mentioned in chapter 7, this is a reprinting of the 1881–2 edition with appendices and a handful of minor typographical corrections) is a result of a theoretical commitment to presenting Whitman's final intentions for his poetry. The Variorum reprints the poems of the "deathbed" edition in chronological order: first the poems of the 1855 edition, then the poems new to the 1856 edition, then those new to the 1860, and so on. The Variorum is intended of course to present more than one edition, though the multiple texts it offers have to be, as it were, supplied by the reader, who must decode and reconstruct them from arcane symbols and abbreviations. The economics of print publishing probably left no other choice, yet what is finally offered to the reader is far removed from anything Whitman ever produced, and it is cumbersome to use.

Unlike the *Collected Writings*, the *Walt Whitman Archive* has not chosen to privilege one particular edition of *Leaves of Grass*. Instead, the editors of the *Whitman Archive* value and seek to present all versions, including all six distinct American editions, the British editions that Whitman contributed to in his lifetime, corrected page proofs, and the famous "Blue Book" – Whitman's copy of the 1860 edition of *Leaves of Grass* with handwritten corrections and with material tipped in. Whitman authorized every published edition of *Leaves of Grass*. Any one of his editions could be vital for a researcher, depending on the questions to be pursued. A student concerned with the poet's reaction to the prospect of black suffrage, for example, might well find the often-neglected 1867 *Leaves* to be crucial. Whitman called for future reprintings based on the "deathbed" edition, saying that it should supersede all the previous editions. To follow his advice would be problematic in numerous ways, especially since it would occlude some of his finest achievements, and it would trust that his judgment of his own work was sharpest in the final year of his life as his health was failing. In the last analysis, we are not editing Whitman *for* Whitman but for ourselves and for all those interested in him in our historical moment.

The most glaring shortcoming in the *Collected Writings* volumes is the omission of Whitman's poetry manuscript notes and drafts. As we have explained in earlier chapters, these are key documents in American literary history that have never before been systematically gathered, transcribed, and edited. Whitman left behind an extraordinary number of manuscripts, which allow us to track the development of his major lifelong work, *Leaves of Grass*. Scattered as fragments in over 70 archives, his manuscripts provide the opportunity to trace the origins of some of America's most innovative and important poetry. Because the poetic drafts are often surrounded by Whitman's notes about events and people he was encountering, these drafts also allow us to track the cultural, historical, and biographical bases of the work. For these reasons, a great portion of the initial work on the *Whitman Archive* has focused on editing the poetry manuscripts.

That work is well underway, though the vastness and complexity of the record Whitman left means that much remains to be done. The *Archive* has gathered and processed approximately 4,000 high-resolution digital images of Whitman's poetry manuscripts. These images can be greatly magnified and otherwise manipulated, sometimes allowing us to detect information that escapes the naked eye. For example, magnification and manipulation of images have enabled us to recover many erased words – in fact entire lines – on one particular "Calamus" manuscript, revealing that Whitman had discussed "lovers" but then erased that word and substituted the less explicit word "comrades." Infrared photography or other related techniques may enable us to recover verso writing that is currently inaccessible because some manuscripts were pasted onto backing sheets, presumably by collectors or by curators early in the twentieth century. The *Archive* is now addressing the technical challenges of providing scaleable images that will allow future users to closely examine any portion of a manuscript.

The *Collected Writings*, in addition to neglecting the poetry manuscripts, also omitted the revelatory periodical printings of Whitman's poems, which are now being edited for the *Archive* by Susan Belasco. Whitman published approximately 150 poems in over forty different periodicals. These documents provide crucial insights into how the poet marketed his writings, how he interacted with editors, and how he extended his audience. The *Whitman Archive* will therefore be the first place the full histories of his poetic composition will be available. Many poems can only be truly understood if readers are presented with the periodical printings as a key part of those histories.

The case of Whitman's familiar poem "A Noiseless Patient Spider" illustrates how complex a poem's development can be. Before it appeared in his *Passage to India* book experiment and was incorporated into the 1881–2 *Leaves of Grass*, this poem had already existed in several earlier forms: prose and verse drafts, as well as a periodical variant. The poem has its origins, as do many of Whitman's poems, in prose jottings he made in a notebook. In this case, the originating passage is found in a notebook that dates to the late 1850s and early 1860s:

> First I wish you to realize well that our boasted knowledge, precious and manifold as it is, sinks into niches and corners, before the infinite knowledge of the unknown. Of the real world of materials, what, after all, are these specks we call knowledge? – Of the spiritual world I announce to you this – much gibberish will always be offered and for a season obeyed – all lands, all times – the soul will yet feel – but to make a statement eludes us – By curious indirections only can there be any statement of the spiritual world – and they will all be foolish – Have you noticed the [worm] on a twig reaching out in the immense vacancy time and again, trying point after point? Not more helplessly does the tongue or the pen of man, essay out in the spiritual spheres, to state them. In the nature of things nothing less than the special world itself can know itself. (*NUPM*, 6:2051)

Here we see Whitman working with a philosophical idea, about how the "spiritual world" can be accessed from the material world, how the vast regions of the unknown can be indicated by language, "the tongue or the pen of man." To ground the philosophical investigation, he hits upon a tentative image – he puts in brackets the word "worm" and imagines a silkworm putting forth filaments.

The image would stay with Whitman over the years and would emerge again during the Civil War, when the ideas he had been ruminating about suddenly manifested themselves in a draft of a poem, written on a page in one of his Civil War notebooks, amidst notes from his visits to wounded soldiers. Here, the "[worm]" has become a spider, an analog of the soul, "throwing out filament after filament," but the poem now shifts surprisingly into a set of images and ideas much more related to his "Calamus" poems about "manly love," and the vastness that the spider/soul is exploring is not the spiritual world or the unknown so much as "the fathomless oceans of love." The poem ends on a moving cry for "latent souls of love – / You pent and unknown oceans of love!" This draft, then, is an early version of "A Noiseless Patient Spider," but it is also closely related to his poems exploring sexuality and desire, poems like "From Pent-up Aching Rivers" and "I Am He That Aches with Love." In the draft, we can see the poet reaching, throwing out lines and filaments into the unknown as he seeks to attach his quest to language. In one place a tantalizingly incomplete line, "as the the," abandons the object and leaves language hanging on the promontory, incomplete:

The Soul, reaching throwing out for love.
As the spider, ~~on a~~ from some little promontory, throwing out filament
   after filament, tirelessly ~~from~~ out of itself, that one at least may catch,
   and form a link, a bridge, a connection
as the the
O I saw one passing alone, ~~and silent~~ saying hardly a word, yet full of
   love I detected him by certain signs
O eyes ever wishfully turning! O silent eyes!
~~O thou eyes turning [illegible] street~~
For then I thought of you oer the world O ~~the~~ latent oceans, fathomless
   ~~sweet~~ oceans of love!
~~The~~ O waiting oceans of love! ~~the~~ yearning and fervid! ~~O~~ and of you
   sweet souls perhaps for the future, delicious and long:

Ð But Dead, unknown on this earth – ungiven, dark here [illegible],
unspoken, never born:
Those You fathomless latent souls of love – those you pent and
unknown oceans of love! (Notebook 94, Harned-Whitman Collection,
Library of Congress)

In 1868 Whitman finally published the poem in *Broadway Magazine*,
as one of several untitled poems in a group called "Whispers of Heavenly Death." Here, the poem is close to what it would be in its final
form in *Leaves of Grass*, but still with some key differences in punctu-
ation. In the periodical version, the casting of the spider/soul is still
tentative, broken again and again by commas: "I mark'd, where, on a
little promontory, it stood, isolated." In the final version, Whitman's
"exploration" – his "crying out," as the etymology of the word suggests
– becomes dominant, erasing the pauses, the separations, as the poem
enacts the casting out of long, seamless filament/lines: "I mark'd where
on a little promontory it stood isolated, ..." Once again, all of these
changes – which are many, often subtle, and which move us from the
ur-poem to the familiar final version – are invisible in the Variorum
of the *Collected Writings*. Our work in progress on the *Whitman Archive*
is designed to allow students and scholars for the first time to track
such illuminating shifts and revisions and fracturings in Whitman's
poems as they move from originating ideas, often in prose notebooks,
to drafts of poems that often led to several different published poems,
to periodical publications that are sometimes close to the final version
but contain key differences. The manuscripts and periodical versions
of all of Whitman's poems are steps in a compositional evolution –
crucial steps for this poet who based his poetics on evolution, on faith
in an ongoing process of life, democracy, and poetry – that an electronic
edition can explore in its entirety.

As a result of an unannounced but profoundly important theoretical
commitment to singularity and the individual author, the *Collected
Writings* routinely omitted work that could be thought of as collaborative. One exception to this generalization is worth noting. *Rambles
Among Words* was printed in Edward Grier's edition of Whitman's
Notebooks and Unpublished Prose Manuscripts. Following the lead of
C. Carroll Hollis, Grier concluded that Whitman had a hand in this text
by William Swinton, though it is by no means certain that Whitman
wrote any of this text at all (Folsom 1986, 290). (Indisputably, as a

published book, it is neither a notebook nor an unpublished prose manuscript, so it is in any case an odd item to include in this section of the *Collected Writings*.) In short, a piece that Whitman just possibly wrote collaboratively was included in the *Collected Writings*, while many other texts that he definitely wrote collaboratively are excluded altogether.

As a range of theorists and textual scholars have variously demonstrated, the idea of an individual, autonomous author is open to significant challenge, and the term *author*, if we are to use it now, might be best understood as a convenient shorthand marker for the many agents – a writer or writers, editors, typesetters, proofreaders, and others – who typically contribute to the production of a text. Whitman himself recognized that texts are rarely the product of a single individual. After the publication of the 1881–2 *Leaves of Grass*, he commented on the importance of his proof-reader's work:

> All this is not only to show my obligation to Henry Clark, but in some sort to all proof-readers everywhere, as sort of a tribute to a class of men, seldom mentioned, but to whom all the hundreds of writers, and all the millions of readers, are unspeakably indebted. More than one literary reputation, if not made is certainly saved by no less a person than a good proof-reader. The public that sees these neat and consecutive, fair-printed books on the centre-tables, little knows the mass of chaos, bad spelling and grammar, frightful (corrected) excesses or balks, and frequent masses of illegibility and tautology of which they have been extricated. (*DBN*, 1:256)

No one would claim that Henry Clark was the equal of Whitman in the making of *Leaves of Grass*, but he contributed to the social production of his text.

The editors of the *Collected Writings*, despite printing the passage above, did little to acknowledge printers and proofreaders (in fact they erased in large measure the contributions of printers). The *Collected Writings* is committed to solitary authorship, and the consequences of this view are enormous. Intellectual content produced jointly by Whitman and others did not fit this model and hence was not represented. To be sure, complicated questions arise when considering the biographies that were partially ghost-written by Whitman, though they appeared under the names of John Burroughs and Richard Maurice Bucke. However, these complications are not sufficient reason to justify excluding this Whitman-mediated material from the record of Whitman's writings. Similarly complicated questions arise again regarding his marginalia, much of it written during the pivotal early phase of his career, some of it trenchant commentary on poetry and poetics. How exactly should we conceive of such writing? Perhaps it should be thought of as a multi-authorial but non-collaborative production (non-collaborative since the writer of the original text in, say, a magazine was an unwitting participant in Whitman's creation of a new text) that depends on an original document *and* a reaction to that document. The *Whitman Archive* anticipates that the marginalia will be included as time and resources allow.

Horace Traubel's *With Walt Whitman in Camden* – the 5,000-page record of Traubel's daily conversations with the poet – raises related questions. Is this nine-volume work published sporadically over a ninety-year period a Whitman text, a Traubel text, or a Whitman–Traubel text? Many speakers are quoted in these volumes, either through Traubel's reproduction of documents or through transcribed conversation. (The transcribed conversation was actually recreated from Traubel's memory on the basis of notes he jotted down shortly after returning home from his almost daily visits to Whitman's room.) But no one – not even Traubel himself – is allotted the number of words that are attributed to Whitman here. These volumes, though excluded from the *Collected Writings*, are a treasure trove of Whitman's opinions on all manner of subjects both trivial and important. The Traubel volumes, representing nothing less or more than Whitman's mediated words, need to be included in any encompassing Whitman resource. Matt Cohen is now well along in editing these nine volumes for the *Walt Whitman Archive*. Making these volumes available in an electronically searchable form will be a great benefit to Whitman studies since few libraries have a complete set, and they are cumbersome to use because of their inadequate indexing. The same issues pertain to the many other, shorter interviews conducted with Whitman over his lifetime. These interviews have never been systematically collected and studied. Brett Barney is now editing these items for the *Whitman Archive*, for they too, if read with appropriate caution, can be the source of vitally important information.

Much of Whitman's journalism can be thought of as falling into that same category of jointly produced intellectual work that the editors of the *Collected Writings* regularly ignored. Representation of the journalism has been restricted by previous editors to the newspaper essays that are thought to be authored by Whitman. That is, Herbert Bergman and his co-editors printed the essays, usually anonymous, that they attributed to Whitman. But when Whitman was the editor of the newspaper – for example, in his two-year stint with the *Brooklyn Daily Eagle* – where does "Whitman" stop? Given that he controlled the inclusion and exclusion and layout of material, should his journalism be limited only to Whitman-authored material? To what extent is the entire newspaper one of his intellectual creations, part of what we need to know for a full or ideal assessment of his career? Clearly there is a difference between material Whitman wrote and material that he edited. But both ought to fall within an inclusive presentation of his intellectual contributions.

Like journalism, correspondence is by its nature fundamentally collaborative, and because the *Collected Writings* treats Whitman's correspondence by printing only his outgoing letters, it effectively erases much of the crucial information and context of the exchanges. A one-sided correspondence is inevitably partial and distorted. In the *Collected Writings*, incoming letters are at best quoted in part or rendered via summary in the footnotes. For the first time, the *Whitman Archive* will make available both sides of Whitmans's correspondence. In addition, he wrote letters for soldiers who could not write for themselves because of injury or illiteracy, and the *Archive* also plans to make these letters available.

Is it wise for a digital thematic research collection to try to include everything Whitman ever wrote and much that has been written about him? As John Unsworth notes, one problem of digital editing is that "the medium seems to elicit scholarly hubris: an infinite amount of material can be stored here, sorted, analyzed and retrieved instantly, provided only that decades of grinding labor have made it all possible, that all the rights have been cleared, and that no fatal mistakes were made, years ago, when the project was designed" (Unsworth 2000, online). Amassing vast amounts of material does not guarantee either clarity or usefulness. That material needs to be transcribed and described in ways that allow for internal integration and easy navigability, presented in a coherent way, and made accessible through search engines and by other means. Masses of data can obscure important information unless the presentation and organization are carefully considered.

The challenges for the *Archive* are to present a huge amount of material from incidental to profound, to render it accurately, and to develop effective means of using electronic tools to organize a vast resource in ways that will be accessible rather than overwhelming. The *Archive* also finds itself with – and welcomes – a large and diverse audience. If a scholarly print edition had a predictably confined audience, a freely available website on a well-known figure like Whitman does not. Like some other large electronic "archives," the *Whitman Archive* is used in classrooms from junior high school to graduate school and has thousands of users from all over the globe.

We said above that one ambition of the *Collected Writings* was to gather in one place "all of Whitman's writings." That is, of course, a deceptively simple remark. The question of what constitutes "all of Whitman's writings" is in fact quite complicated. The editors of the *Collected Writings* discussed this point:

> At first the editorial staff hoped to print everything, so that the *Collected Writings* could be called absolutely "complete." But some items . . . will probably continue to come to light for years to come. Moreover, many of the miscellaneous manuscripts are hardly more than lists of words, names, address[es], trial titles, and trivial memoranda. Is a poet's laundry list worth publishing? This is not a rhetorical question, for maybe it should be. But the question is still being debated by the editors of the *Collected Writings* and the New York University Press. (quoted in Folsom 1982, 70)

With regard to the *Notebooks and Unpublished Prose Manuscripts* and the *Daybooks and Notebooks*, it seems that the principle of their editors, Edward Grier and William White, was to publish all scraps of prose writing in Whitman's hand, presumably on the grounds that he is one of those writers of such rare importance that every conceivable bit of evidence about him is worth retaining and recording. But there are inexplicable omissions: for example, why are we given an entire entry for the offhand notation "I am writing this at Providence, where there is a long wait" when things as important as Whitman's wills are excluded?

Electronic editing has some disadvantages (including unresolved questions regarding preservation), but digital technologies also provide some significant advantages that are worth considering. Specifically, the *Whitman Archive* is involved in the tagging of documents – the application of computer-readable markers to describe textual features – that will eventually enable users to perform sophisticated research on the documents we include. The tagging that enriches documents in the *Whitman Archive* is ordinarily invisible to users when they view them through a standard web browser. A thorough discussion of the *Archive*'s technical practices is not possible here, but a general explanation of how tagging enables scholarship is useful in further distinguishing print and digital projects. (Those interested in the *Whitman Archive* tagging practices can consult encoding guidelines at www.whitmanarchive.org/guidelines.) Our project uses a customized implementation of XML (eXtensible Markup Language) to flag important textual features of Whitman's manuscripts, indicating, for example, that a certain string of text is a title rather than a poetic line or a paragraph. This type of mark-up will allow users to quickly gather useful, reliable facts, such as the frequency of "America" in his titles or the number of drafts in which he mentions the soul or the prairies or prostitutes. Other aspects of our tagging will allow scholars to derive reliable information about Whitman's revising processes and artistic development: it will be possible to discover how often he changed the word "poem" to "song," examine all instances in which he revised "lover" to "comrade," calculate how often he numbered stanzas, or locate and compare his uses of the word "death" in poems from two different periods of his career. Formerly, such scholarship involving thousands of manuscripts spread among dozens of institutions would have been unreliable and career-consuming at best, and most likely simply impossible.

An electronic edition also has the power to give multiple views of the same object. The *Whitman Archive*, for example, describes a poetry manuscript through the use of Encoded Archival Description (EAD), transcribes the text so that it is compliant with the Text Encoding Initiative (TEI), and provides a digital surrogate for the original through a high-quality color scan or a digital photograph. Each is an important representation of the original artifact, and each provides different kinds of information. It was not feasible, for example, for the editors of the *Collected Writings* to reproduce in facsimile more than an occasional sample of the source material underlying their edition. This is a genuine possibility with an electronic edition, given adequate financing and cooperation from repositories. Users can check the work of *Archive*

editors, see the basis of editorial decisions, and offer suggested corrections. The *Archive*'s critics become the editors' collaborators.

The *Whitman Archive*, then, allows us to see Whitman anew, re-
scripted in ways informed by recent developments in editorial theory
and textual scholarship. Accordingly, the *Archive* editors are more
attentive to what Jerome McGann has called "bibliographic codes"
than were the editors of the *Collected Writings* (McGann 1991, 57).
Throughout his career Whitman designed covers and bindings, chose
fonts and ornaments, controlled layout, and inserted photographs –
these features were integral components of the poetic effects he worked
to achieve. With regard to the 1881–2 *Leaves of Grass*, he explained
that he wanted the famous image of himself with arm akimbo, which
had appeared as the frontispiece in the first edition (reproduced above
as figure 4), to now face "Song of Myself" because the portrait "is
involved as part of the poem." And with regard to the "deathbed"
edition he requested that future editors present not just his words but
a "facsimile" of this text. In their treatment of Whitman's poetry, the
editors of the *Collected Writings* honor his line breaks, but in other
regards they ignore his sense of the visual; textual expressiveness is
limited to the semantic content. The *Whitman Archive* is able to present
both searchable etext and facsimiles of all the editions by means of its
digital surrogates for the originals. Covers, bindings, and front matter,
though excluded from the *Collected Writings*, can be included in an
electronic edition. Users can study not only Whitman's words, but the
fonts he chose to display those words in.

As John Lavagnino has remarked:

> It is impossible for a transcription to reproduce the original object;
> it's always a selection of features from that object: the words but not
> their size on the page or the depth of the chisel marks, major changes
> in type style but not variations in the ink's darkness from page to page
> or over time. Any such features that do seem essential for a particular
> transcription can be encoded; what's impossible is notating every
> observable feature. (Lavagnino forthcoming)

The *Archive* encoding is primarily based on non-controversial structural
aspects of Whitman's documents: lines, line groups, titles, and so on.
But even these apparently self-evident units are hardly self-evident
in particular curious cases that appear regularly. Given the size of the

Whitman corpus, the editors have not noted all the information about manuscripts, some of which is no doubt important: paper type, inks, and pinholes, among other matters. These physical features of manuscripts provide potentially illuminating avenues for inquiry. As editors, we have judged, however, that we should invest our limited time recording other information that seems to us even more important. Fortunately, tagging can be a reiterative process, and what hasn't been tagged on a first pass, by us with our interests, could be tagged later by others, who could build on our initial transcriptions and tagging.

The *Whitman Archive* has, in the first nine years of its existence, accomplished about 20 percent of the work described in this chapter. Given the magnitude of what the *Whitman Archive* could be, it is important to think from an early stage about the possibility of handing the project over in the future. Fortunately the *Whitman Archive* is already a multi-generational undertaking that, we hope, can be built upon, migrated to new formats as software evolves, and refreshed. As previously indicated, we are documenting our editing practices extensively, so that later editors will understand what we did and why. Unlike print editions of the past that generally rejected previous work in order to start afresh, we are trying to create a resource that can be passed on to later scholars and continuously improved. An electronic edition, unlike a print edition, is typically issued as work in progress rather than as a finished product. As it is made public, its readers become active agents in its continuing creation – pointing out omissions, suggesting improvements, challenging transcriptions. The *Archive* is revised and expanded virtually every day, and newly discovered documents can be seamlessly folded into the existing structures so that the edition is always up to date. It is the perfect medium for an author who was always revising and reordering and rethinking his work. As editors, we are confident that the *Archive* will keep the re-scripting of Whitman active for generations hence.

References

Asselineau, Roger. *The Evolution of Walt Whitman: The Creation of a Personality*, 2 vols. (Cambridge, MA: Belknap Press of Harvard University Press, 1960, 1962).

Barrus, Clara. *Whitman and Burroughs: Comrades* (Boston: Houghton Mifflin, 1931).

Baym, Nina, general ed. *The Norton Anthology of American Literature*. Vol. 1 (New York: W. W. Norton, 1994).

Bowers, Fredson, ed. *Whitman's Manuscripts: Leaves of Grass (1860)* (Chicago: University of Chicago Press, 1955).

Brenton, James J., ed. *Voices from the Press* (New York: Charles B. Norton, 1850).

Bucke, Richard Maurice. *Walt Whitman* (Philadelphia: David McKay, 1883).

Bucke, Richard Maurice, ed. *Calamus: A Series of Letters Written During the Years 1868–1880 by Walt Whitman to a Young Friend (Peter Doyle)* (Boston: Laurens Maynard, 1897).

Burroughs, John. *Notes on Walt Whitman as Poet and Person* (New York: J. S. Redfield, 1867).

Ceniza, Sherry. *Walt Whitman and 19th-Century Women Reformers* (Tuscaloosa: University of Alabama Press, 1998).

Emerson, Ralph Waldo. *Essays and Lectures* (New York: Literary Classics of the United States, 1983).

Erkkila, Betsy. "Whitman and the Homosexual Republic." In Ed Folsom, ed., *Walt Whitman: The Centennial Essays* (Iowa City: University of Iowa Press, 1994).

Folsom, Ed. "The Whitman Project: A Review Essay." *Philological Quarterly* 61 (1982), 369–94.

Folsom, Ed. Review of Walt Whitman, *Notebooks and Unpublished Prose Manuscripts*, ed. Edward Grier. *Philological Quarterly* 65 (1986), 287–91.

Glicksberg, Charles I., ed. *Walt Whitman and the Civil War.* 1933. Rpt. (New York: Barnes, 1963).

Haven, Cynthia L. "Man of Letters." *Washington Post Book World* (August 8, 2004), 13.

Higginson, Thomas Wentworth. "Women and Men: War Pensions for Women." *Harper's Bazaar* (March 5, 1887), 162.

Hutchinson, George B. *The Ecstatic Whitman* (Columbus: Ohio State University Press, 1986).

Hutchinson, George B. "Life Review and the Common World in Whitman's *Specimen Days.*" *South Atlantic Review* 52 (November, 1987), 3–23.

Ingersoll, Robert Green. *Fifty Great Selections* (New York: C. P. Farrell, 1920).

Jaén, Didier Tisdel, trans. *Homage to Walt Whitman: A Collection of Poems from the Spanish* (University, AL: University of Alabama Press, 1969).

Kaplan, Justin. "The Naked Self and Other Problems." In Marc Pachter, ed., *Telling Lives: The Biographer's Art* (Washington, DC: New Republic Books, 1979).

Kaplan, Justin. *Walt Whitman: A Life* (New York: Simon and Schuster, 1980).

Katz, Jonathan Ned. *Love Stories: Sex between Men before Homosexuality* (Chicago: University of Chicago Press, 2001).

Krieg, Joan. "Without Walt Whitman in Camden." *Walt Whitman Quarterly Review* 14 (1996–7), 85–112.

Lavagnino, John. "When Not to Use TEI." In Lou Burnard, Katherine O'Brien O'Keeffe, and John Unsworth, eds., *Electronic Textual Editing* (New York: Modern Language Association, forthcoming).

Loving, Jerome. *Walt Whitman's Champion: William Douglas O'Connor.* (College Station: Texas A&M University Press, 1978).

Martin, Robert K., ed. *The Continuing Presence of Walt Whitman* (Iowa City: University of Iowa Press, 1992).

McGann, Jerome. *The Textual Condition* (Princeton, NJ: Princeton University Press, 1991).

Murray, Martin. "Traveling with the Wounded: Walt Whitman and Washington's Civil War Hospitals." *Washington History* 8 (1996–7), 58–73, 92–93.

Myerson, Joel, ed. *Whitman in His Own Time* (Detroit: Omnigraphics, 1991).

Olsen-Smith, Steven, and Hershel Parker. "'Live Oak, with Moss' and 'Calamus': Textual Inhibitions in Whitman Criticism." *Walt Whitman Quarterly Review* 14 (1997), 153–65.

Palmer, Carole. "Thematic Research Collections." In Susan Schreibman, Ray Siemens, and John Unsworth, eds. *A Companion to Digital Humanities* (Oxford: Blackwell, 2004).

Parker, Hershel. "The Real 'Live Oak, with Moss': Straight Talk about Whitman's 'Gay Manifesto.'" *Nineteenth-Century Literature* 51 (1996), 145–60.

Perlman, Jim, Dan Campion, and Ed Folsom, eds. *Walt Whitman: The Measure of His Song* (Duluth: Holy Cow! Press, 1998).

Price, Kenneth M. "Whitman's Solutions to 'The Problem of the Blacks.'" *Resources for American Literary Study* 15 (1985), 205–208.

Salveson, Paul. "Loving Comrades: Lancashire's Links to Walt Whitman." *Walt Whitman Quarterly Review* 14 (1996–7), 57–84.

Sanborn, Franklin Benjamin. "Reminiscent of Whitman." In Joel Myerson, ed., *Whitman in His Own Time* (Iowa City: University of Iowa Press, 2000).

Shephard, Esther. "Possible Sources of Some of Whitman's Ideas and Symbols in *Hermes Mercurius Trismegistus* and Other Works." *Modern Language Quarterly* 14 (1953), 62–81.

Smith-Rosenberg, Carroll. *Disorderly Conduct: Visions of Gender in Victorian America* (New York: Oxford University Press, 1986).

Stern, Madeleine B. *Heads and Headlines: The Phrenological Fowlers* (Norman: University of Oklahoma Press, 1971).

Traubel, Horace, ed. *Camden's Compliment to Walt Whitman* (Philadelphia: David McKay, 1889).

Traubel, Horace, Richard Maurice Bucke, and Thomas B. Harned, eds. *In Re Walt Whitman* (Philadelphia: David McKay, 1893).

Unsworth, John. "The Importance of Failure." *Journal of Electronic Publishing* 3 (December, 1997). www.press.umich.edu/jep/03-02/unsworth.html. Accessed October 7, 2004.

Unsworth, John. "Second-Generation Digital Resources in the Humanities." www.iath.virginia.edu/%7Ejmu2m/DRH2000.html. Accessed October 8, 2004.

Index

abolitionist writers 61, 70–1, 75
African Americans 3, 75, 86, 101,
    102–3
  see also black subjectivity; black
    suffrage; slavery
"After All Not to Create Only" 101
Akin, Amanda 85
Alboni, Marietta 11
Alcott, Bronson 60
Alcott, Louisa May 87
Alexie, Sherman 129
"Ambition" 14
American Revolution 2
Anaya, Rudolfo 129
Aristotle 113, 114–15
Arnold, George 61
Ashton, J. Hubley 94
Asselineau, Roger 28

"Backward Glance O'er Travel'd
    Roads, A" 127
Bacon, Delia 119
Banner at Day-Break 75
Barney, Brett 140
baseball 97
Baxter, Sylvester 122
"Beat! Beat! Drums!" 80
Belasco, Susan 136

Benjamin, Park 9
Bergman, Herbert 141
Binns, Henry Bryan 13
black subjectivity 52, 54, 55
black suffrage 101, 102, 103, 104
Bliss, D. Willard 85
bodily emphasis 44–6, 48, 71, 72,
    79, 80
book and identity, conflation of 5,
    21–2
book production xii, 21–2
Booth, John Wilkes 93
Booth, Junius 6
Borges, Jorge Luis 47
Boston 71, 117
"Boston Ballad, A" 23
Bowers, Fredson 63
Brenton, James J. 16
Brooklyn 3, 77
Brooklyn Eagle 11–12, 141
"Brooklyniana" 77
Brown, Henry Kirke 60
Brown, John 70–1, 124
Brown, Lewis 89
Bryant, William Cullen 14, 19, 120
Buchanan, Robert 106
Bucke, Richard Maurice 26, 27, 28,
    29, 85, 120, 130, 139

Burroughs, John 26, 85, 87, 92, 108, 139
"By Blue Ontario's Shore" 118
"By the Roadside" 110
Byron, Lord George 19

"Calamus" 62–3, 65, 66–8, 69, 72, 73, 79, 85, 93, 118, 126, 135–6
Camden 104, 105, 116, 121–2, 125
Carlyle, Thomas 12, 101, 104, 120
Carpenter, Edward 115–16
catalogs 45, 49, 59, 95–7
Cattell, Edward 64, 107
Cauldwell, William 10
Ceniza, Sherry 61
Centennial (1876) 105–6
"Chants Democratic and Native American" 73
"Child's Amaze, A" 110
"Child's Champion, The" 10
"Children of Adam" 69
  see also "Enfans d'Adam"
Childs, George W. 121
Chopin, Kate 119
Civil War xiv, 2, 11, 54, 64, 76–91, 92, 95–7
Clapp, Henry 61
Clare, Ada 61
Clark, Henry 139
"Clear the way there Jonathan" 25
Cohen, Matt 140
Coleridge, Samuel Taylor 19
collaborative work 138–9
The Collected Writings of Walt Whitman x–xi, xv, 131–3, 134, 135, 136, 138, 139, 141, 142, 144
Complete Writings of Walt Whitman xv, 130, 131
Comstock, Anthony 117
Conway, Moncure 61, 99
Cooper, James Fenimore 6
correspondence 141

Crescent (New Orleans) 12, 14
crossing, act of 3, 78
"Crossing Brooklyn Ferry" 3, 59

Daily Standard (Brooklyn) 77
Daily Times (Brooklyn) 61
"Dalliance of the Eagles, The" 118
Davis, Paulina Wright 61
Daybooks and Notebooks 142
"Death of the Nature-Lover" 14
"Death in the School-Room" 9
democratic ideas and poetics ix–x, 18, 45, 46, 47–8, 49, 67, 68–9, 71, 79, 101–2
Democratic party 7, 18
Democratic Review 8, 9
democratic virtue 110, 111, 114
Democratic Vistas xiv, 100, 101–2, 103–4, 130
Dewey, John 101
Dickens, Charles 117
Donaldson, Thomas 122
Dowden, Edward 106
Doyle, Peter 64, 83, 92–4, 107, 108, 115, 128, 130
Drum-Taps xiv, 80, 82, 89–90, 91, 98, 99, 103
Duckett, Bill 64, 115, 122

Eakins, Thomas 105
educational philosophy 3–4, 7, 9
Eldridge, Charles 70, 71, 76, 84
electronic editing 142–3
Emerson, Ralph Waldo 12, 22, 25, 56, 58, 59, 60, 71, 84, 117, 120
"Enfans d'Adam" 68, 71, 72, 73
English readership 99–100, 107, 126
Erkkila, Betsy 67
"Europe: The 72d and 73d Years of These States" 23

"Faces" 23, 118
"Father Taylor (and Oratory)" 124
Faulkner, William 129
fiction 8–10, 16
    short stories 16
    see also *Franklin Evans; or*
        The Inebriate
"First O Songs for Prelude" 80
Fowler, Lorenzo 15, 16
Fowler, Orson 16
Fowler and Wells 16, 57
Franklin Evans; or The Inebriate 9–10
Fred Gray Association 62
friendships
    virtuous 114–15
    women 60–1, 107
    working-class 78, 92–3, 107
    writers and artists 60, 61, 87
    see also relationships
Fritzinger, Warren 64, 115, 128
"From Pent-up Aching Rivers" 118,
    137
Fuller, Margaret 118

Gardner, Alexander 87
gay identity 64, 65, 66, 73
    see also homosexuality; male–male
        affection
gender-role fluidity 85
genius 58
Genoways, Ted 132
Gilchrist, Alexander 107
Gilchrist, Anne Burrows 107
Gilchrist, Herbert 107
Gilman, Charlotte Perkins 119
Ginsberg, Allen 129
Gold, Michael 129
"the good life" 109, 110, 111–13,
    114, 115
Good-Bye My Fancy 124
graveyard school of English poetry
    14

"Great Are the Myths" 23
Grier, Edward 26, 138, 142

Harlan, James 94, 95
Harned, Thomas 128, 130
Harrison, Gabriel 42, 60
Hartshorne, William 5
Hawley, Harriet Foote 85
Hawthorne, Nathaniel 117
Hayes, A. H. 12
Helms, Alan 64, 65–6
Hicks, Elias 4
Higginson, Thomas Wentworth 85,
    122–4
Hine, Charles 69
Hollyer, Samuel 42
homoeroticism 62
homosexuality 8, 64–5, 66, 67–8,
    73, 115, 126
    see also gay identity; male–male
        affection
Hongo, Garrett 129
hospital visits 77–9, 92, 102
Howells, William Dean 61
Hughes, Langston 129
"Hush'd Be the Camps To-day"
    91
Hutchinson, George 37–8, 120

"I Am He That Aches with Love"
    137
"I Dream'd in a Dream" 68–9
"I Sing the Body Electric" 13, 23,
    118
Indian Bureau 90–1
Ingersoll, Robert Green 108, 111

Jackson, Andrew 1
Johnson, Andrew 102
Johnston, Dr John 126
Jordan, June 129
juvenilia 25

Kaplan, Justin xii
Katz, Jonathan Ned 63, 64
Keats, John 19
Kennedy, William Sloane 122
Kertbeny, Karl Maria 64–5
Komunyakaa, Yusef 129

Lafayette, General 2
Lavagnino, John 144
Lawrence, D. H. 118
Leaves of Grass
  binding 41–2, 58, 74–5
  composition and revision 25–40,
    70
  critical reception 56, 59, 75
  editions
    1855 edition xi, xiii, 16, 22,
      23–9, 41–2, 44–5, 48, 56, 57,
      112–13
    1856 edition 57–9
    1860 edition 68–70, 74–5, 76
    1867 edition xiv, 98–9, 135
    1871 edition 48, 99
    1881 edition 117–18, 127, 144
    Centennial Edition (1876) 42,
      106
    "deathbed" edition xi, 127,
      130, 134, 135, 144
    Variorum Edition xi, 25, 134
  genesis 25–7
  key vocabulary 15
  manuscript sources xi, xiii, 17–18,
    22–3, 25–6, 30–7, 50–4, 66,
    137–8
  "missing manuscript" 28
  organizational plan 23, 24, 25
  reordering and rebuilding xiv, 92,
    99
  riddle of the grass 37–9
  sales 56, 59, 75
  suppression controversy 118, 124
  working titles 23, 48, 59

Lee, Robert E. 80, 91
Leech, Abraham 7
L'Enfant, Pierre 86
Lincoln, Abraham 12, 76, 85, 87,
  91, 93, 121
Lincoln lectures 121
Linton, William 106
"Live Oak, with Moss" 62, 63, 64,
  65–6
Long Island 4
Long Island Democrat 16
Long Island Star 11
Long Islander 8
Longaker, Daniel 128
Longfellow, Henry Wadsworth 71,
  120
love poems xiii, 62–3, 64, 65–8, 69
"Love That Is Hereafter, The" 14
Lovering, Henry B. 122

McClure, J. E. 12
McGann, Jerome 144
McKay, David 118, 121
male–male affection 15, 49, 62,
  63–4, 65, 67, 83, 85, 115, 118
  see also gay identity;
    homosexuality
"Marches now the War is Over"
  99
marginalia 14, 140
Marsh, William 11
mass death 95–7
materiality of printed objects xii, 5
Memoranda During the War xiv, 38,
  87–8, 95–7, 105, 106, 119
"Memorandum at a Venture" 118
Merrill, George 115
"Messenger Leaves" 73
Miller, Edwin Haviland 132
"Million Dead, Too, Summ'd Up,
  The" 95–7
miscegenation 10

Missouri Compromise 2
Muybridge, Eadweard 105
"My Tribute to Four Poets" 120
mysticism 121

Native Americans 90–1, 125
"Native Moments" 118
"New Bible," creation of 74, 79, 82
New Orleans 13, 18
New York Times 88, 90
"Noiseless Patient Spider, A" 136–8
notebooks 17–18, 26, 30, 33, 35,
    36, 136, 137
*Notebooks and Unpublished Prose
    Manuscripts* 17–18, 26, 142
November Boughs 124

"O Captain! My Captain!" 91, 121
O'Brien, Fitz-James 61
O'Connor, William Douglas 70, 75,
    79, 84, 85, 90, 94–5, 104, 118
Olsen-Smith, Steven 65
"Once I Pass'd through a Populous
    City" 13
opera 11
"Osceola" 91, 124, 125
Osgood, James 117, 118
"Our Future Lot" 14
"Out of the Cradle Endlessly
    Rocking" 4, 11, 61, 65, 73

Paine, Thomas 2
Parker, Hershel 65, 66
"Passage to India" 100, 101
Passage to India 100, 136
Patriot (Long Island) 5
personalism 102
Pfaff's saloon 61, 62, 87
Philadelphia 105
philosophical investigation 113,
    137
photography 105, 112

phrenological reading 15, 16
"Pictures" 31
Poe, Edgar Allan 120
Poems by Walt Whitman 99–100
poetry
    anti-slavery statements 50–5
    black subjectivity 52, 54, 55
    bodily emphasis 44–6, 48, 71, 72,
        79, 80
    catalogs 45, 49, 59, 95–7
    cluster arrangements 65, 73–4
    democratic ideas ix–x, 18, 45, 46,
        47–8, 49, 67, 68–9, 71, 79,
        101–2
    free verse 18, 25, 44
    intimacy of the reading
        experience 46–8, 72–3
    love poems xiii, 62–3, 64, 65–8,
        69
    poetic education 14
    public act 70
    radical poetics x, 17, 18, 19, 21,
        22, 42, 44, 47–8
    rural and urban settings 4
    see also specific titles
"Poets to Come" 128
politics 7, 18, 61, 102
Pound, Ezra 125
"Prayer of Columbus" 104
Pretor, Alfred 126–7
Price, Abby 61
print technology xii–xiii
proofreading 139

Quaker beliefs 4

racial attitudes 18–19, 101, 102–4
Rambles Among Words 138–9
Reconstruction era xiv, 92, 99, 102,
    105
Redpath, James 70, 87
Rees Welsh & Co. 118

relationships 62, 64, 92–4, 107–10, 115, 122
  see also friendships
religion 111, 112
Rhys, Ernest 130
"Robert Burns as Poet and Person" 124
Roberts Brothers 100
Romantic poets 19
Rome, Andrew 33
Rossetti, William Michael 99–100, 106, 107, 130
Rousseau, Jean-Jacques 113
Rukeyser, Muriel 129

"Sailing the Mississippi at Midnight" 14
Sand, George 119
"Sands at Seventy" 124
Schmidt, Rudolph 106
Scott, Sir Walter 6
self, celebration of the 19, 21, 46, 115
sensory experience 44–6, 48–9, 72
Sequel to Drum-Taps 91–2, 98
sexual equality 61, 75, 103, 119
sexuality
  female 73, 119
  gender-role fluidity 85
  and the reading experience 72–3
  Whitman's 63, 64, 65, 126, 127
  see also gay identity; homosexuality; male–male affection
"Shadow and the Light of a Young Man's Soul, The" 9
Shephard, Esther 33
"Slang in America" 124
slang words 44
slavery 2, 12, 13, 18–19, 23, 49–50, 55, 113, 114
  abolitionist writers 61, 70–1, 75

slave rebellions 50
  see also "Sleepers, The"
sleep and dreams 48, 49
"Sleepers, The" 23, 48–55, 118
  Lucifer passage 53–4, 55
Smith-Rosenberg, Carroll 63
socialism x, 126, 129
sodomy 8, 64
"Song for Occupations, A" 23
"Song of the Answerer" 23
"Song of the Exposition" 101
"Song of Myself" xii, 7, 16, 21, 23, 25–6, 30–7, 39, 44, 53, 55, 59, 73, 89, 109–10, 118, 144
  manuscripts xii, 30–8
Songs Before Parting 98
"Songs of Insurrection" 99
Southold, New York 8
Specimen Days xiv, 38, 88, 119–20, 130
Speed, James 94
"Spontaneous Me" 118
Stafford, Harry 64, 107–9, 110, 115, 128
Stanton, Elizabeth Cady 119
"Starting from Paumanok" 73, 90–1
Stedman, Edmund Clarence 61
Stevens, Oliver 117
"Sun-Down Poem" 59
suppression controversy 118, 124
Swinton, William 138
Symonds, John Addington 126–7

Taylor, Bayard 105, 106
temperance fiction 9–10
Thayer, William 70, 71, 76
"There Was a Child Went Forth" 7, 23
"This Compost" 59
Thoreau, Henry David 60
"Thought" 111
Timber Creek 107, 120

"To a Certain Cantatrice" 11
"To a Common Prostitute" 110, 118
"To a Foil'd European
    Revolutionaire" 59
"To the Sun-Set Breeze" 124, 125
"To Think of Time" 23, 31
"Tomb Blossoms, The" 16
Traubel, Horace 27, 28, 38, 39, 56,
    114, 125, 126, 127, 128, 130,
    140
Trowbridge, John Townsend 75
Twain, Mark 117
"Twilight Song, A" 124–5
Two Rivulets 106
Tyndale, Sarah 61

Ulrichs, Karl Heinrich 64
"Unfolded Out of the Folds" 118
Unsworth, John 141

Van Anden, Isaac 12
Van Buren, Martin 7
Van Velsor, Amy (grandmother) 4
Van Velsor, Major Cornelius
    (grandfather) 4
Vaughan, Dr Charles 126–7
Vaughan, Fred 62, 64, 93
Vedder, Elihu 60

Wallace, J. W. 126
Walt Whitman Archive x, xv, 30,
    133–6, 138, 140, 141, 142,
    143–5
Washington, D.C. 1, 83, 84, 85–6,
    87, 90, 91
Washington, George 1, 49, 55, 95
Wells, Samuel R. 16
West Hills, New York 1, 56
Wharton, Edith 119
"When Lilacs Last in the Dooryard
    Bloom'd" 91, 92, 121
"Whispers of Heavenly Death" 138

White, William 142
Whitman, Andrew (brother) 2, 3,
    77, 86, 87
Whitman, Edward (brother) 2, 3,
    29, 77, 128
Whitman, George (brother) 2, 8,
    29, 77, 79, 80, 89, 90, 91, 104,
    121, 128
Whitman, Hannah (sister) 2, 3, 86,
    128
Whitman, Jesse (brother) 2, 3, 56,
    77, 86, 90
Whitman, Louisa (sister-in-law)
    104
Whitman, Louisa (mother) 2, 3, 4,
    87, 104, 128
Whitman, Mary (sister) 2
Whitman, Thomas ("Jeff") (brother)
    2, 6, 11, 12, 13, 77, 84, 100,
    120
Whitman, Walt
    autobiography 119–20
    biographies 87, 120–1, 125–6,
        139, 140
    boyhood and education xii, 1,
        3–5, 6
    death and funeral 111, 128
    family background 2–3, 4
    government employment 90–1,
        94
    hospital work 78, 80, 82–3, 84–5,
        86, 87–8, 89, 102, 119
    ill health 89, 93, 94, 104, 119–
        20, 125, 127–8
    journalism 5, 8, 10–12, 61, 77,
        106, 140–1
    journeyman printer xii, 5, 6, 21
    legacy x, 128–9
    portraits 20, 42, 43, 70, 81, 106,
        115, 123
    relationships 62, 64, 92–4,
        107–10, 115, 122

sexuality 63, 64, 65, 126, 127
teaching career xiii, 6–7, 9
writing habits 29
Whitman, Walter (father) 2, 3, 56
Whittier, John Greenleaf 56, 120
"Who Learns My Lesson Complete"
    23
"Wild Frank's Return" 10
Wild, Fred 126
Wilde, Oscar 116
Williams, William Carlos 128
Willis, Sara Payson 61
"Winding-Up, The" 14

With Walt Whitman in Camden
    125–6, 140
"Woman Waits for Me, A" 72–3,
    118, 119
women
    friendships with 60–1
    sexuality 73, 119
    women's rights activists 60–1
Wordsworth, William 19
Worthington, Richard 76
Wright, Frances 6, 7, 119

"Yonnondio" 91